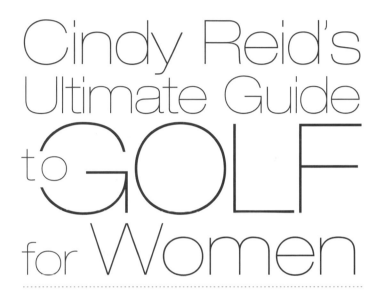

Cindy Reid's Ultimate Guide to GOLF for Women

Cindy Reid's Ultimate Guide to GOLF for Women

CINDY REID
with Steve Eubanks

ATRIA BOOKS

New York London Toronto Sydney Singapore

ATRIA BOOKS

1230 Avenue of the Americas
New York, NY 10020

ISBN: 0-7434-4419-1

First Atria Books hardcover edition May 2003

10 9 8 7 6 5 4 3 2 1

ATRIA BOOKS is a trademark of Simon & Schuster, Inc.

For information regarding special discounts for bulk purchases,
please contact Simon & Schuster Special Sales at 1-800-456-6798
or business@simonandschuster.com

Printed in the U.S.A.

To the most important people in my life:
my parents, Bill and Sylvia Sullivan.
And also to Bill Reid and my
personal fitness trainer, Jody Kraus.

Acknowledgments

Just as learning golf takes a lot of time and the help of a lot of people, writing a book about golf is more time-consuming than I could have ever imagined, and is a team effort in every respect. I owe a great debt of gratitude to my dear friend, student, and publisher, Judith Curr at Atria Books. Without her enthusiasm and encouragement, this project would have never gotten off the lesson tee.

Also, special thanks go out to my editor, Luke Dempsey, one of the great ones in the business. You make the work better, which is a gift. And to my friend and agent, Mark Reiter—remember to keep your hands working together as a single unit and load onto your right side.

My great friend Susan Reed, now editor of *Golf for Women* magazine, was also instrumental in making this project a success; and Bill Reid, who is the director of operations at Teton Springs, gave me the strength and confidence to know I could do this. Others who are owed thanks include Sam Greenwood, Kelly Blackburn, Ed Oldfield, Juleigh Furlong, Jody Kraus, Tim Finchem, and my coauthor, Steve Eubanks, without whom this book would not exist.

Contents

Introduction   I

PART ONE:
Preparing to Play

1   Learning How to Learn   12

2   Making the Game Your Own   33

3   Practice   48

PART TWO:
Fundamentals of the Game

4   Putting: The Game Within the Game   74

5   Gripping the Club: The First Fundamental   100

6   The Setup   114

7   Scoring Shots   136

8   The Full Swing   164

9   Odd Lies (Or "Up the Down Fairway")   208

10   Playing the Game   222

11   Competition and Fun   234

PART THREE:
Beyond the Course

12   Fit for Golf   248

13   Unwritten Rules of the Game   283

Epilogue   297

Index   301

IT WAS A SIMPLE ENOUGH QUESTION, one I should have been able to answer without a breath of hesitation. How had he put it again? "So, Cindy, what qualifies you to be the director of instruction at the TPC at Sawgrass?"

That was easy. I had been a touring professional; I'd learned the game from the best instructors in the world; I'd taught alongside legends. I was as qualified as anyone to take this job. If the question had only been about my curriculum vitae, the answer would have been simple. But the implications of the question were a lot more complicated than that. This wasn't a club member asking me how many golf lessons I'd given in my career or how many good players I'd coached. The question was coming from a PGA Tour player, someone well known

Introduction

in the golf world. Plus, there was an unspoken tone to the question, something that had nothing to do with my qualifications as a golf instructor. He was seemingly asking what qualified me to be the chief teacher at his club, but what he was really saying was, "Why would we hire you to head up instruction at one of the premier clubs in the world when we could hire somebody with the last name of Leadbetter or Harmon? Why hire you when we could have anybody in the world?" He was also indirectly asking about my gender. How could the home club of the PGA Tour hire a woman as its chief teacher?

I had been in plenty of interviews in my life, so I knew what to say. Sitting with my best posture, wearing my best business suit with matching earrings, and smiling throughout, I opened my mouth to give the prepackaged answer I'd been practicing in front of my mirror for a couple of days. Then I hesitated. What *did* qualify me to be sitting here? Why should the greatest golfers in the world hire me to be the director of instruction at their home club? For a brief moment, the question made me think back on where I'd been and what I'd done to reach this point.

"Well," I began, "I believe that in order to be a great teacher you to have to be able to relate to your students. I'm able to do that, because, like many of the people who come to this club for lessons, I didn't take up golf until I was an adult, age twenty-four to be exact. Before that, I was a skier, a basketball player, a fast-pitch softball player, and an elementary school phys-ed teacher. I'd never paid much attention to golf."

In fact, I thought it was a silly game. I couldn't imagine anything more boring than chasing a little white ball around. I'd rather take up cricket or croquet. But I didn't share these views during my interview.

"Elementary-school teachers aren't paid very well," I continued, sharing a view that was news to no one. "In order to pay my rent and make my monthly car payment, I took a part-time job as a beverage cart girl at a local golf club. That's when I first took an interest in the game."

My interest didn't peak immediately—another little detail I chose not to share in this forum. For the first few months I was on the job I couldn't figure out why the men and women I saw every day took such an all-consuming, emotional interest in what appeared on the surface to me to be such a boring game. What was the big deal? The ball was sitting still, for goodness sake. All you had to do was hit it. I'd been a fast-pitch softball player in college, and more than a few of my pitches had been clocked at over ninety miles per hour. Once, during a goof-off afternoon when we were sharing a field with the men's baseball team, I challenged a couple of the guys to try to hit one of my pitches. The team's best hitter gave it a go but didn't have much luck. The fact that his name was Barry Bonds didn't mean much to me at the time. I understood that hitting a moving target was tough, even for the best in the world. But a golf ball was sitting on the ground right in front of you. You had plenty of time to prepare yourself to hit it. How tough could it be?

It wasn't until I tried it for the first time that I realized how wrong I had been. Hitting a golf ball the distance and direction you wanted was one of the toughest athletic feats I'd ever attempted.

The reason I attempted it at all was curiosity. After several months of driving the beverage cart I wondered what all the fuss was about. I was captivated by the amount of fun the people seemed to be having. Not only were they competing in a game they obviously loved, they were having a great time doing it.

That feeling, that competitive charge, was something I sorely missed. I grew up as the ninth of eleven children in a household where you had to compete to survive. My father was a former amateur boxer and my mom had competed as a figure skater, so athletic competition was a part of my life from the time I could walk. Whether it was skipping a rock across a lake, skiing down a slope, or making free throws on the basketball court, I had competed with my siblings since the time I was a toddler. That competitiveness had paid off for me in the form of a college scholarship, as well as a chance to compete on the U.S. Junior National Ski Team. At Arizona State University I played basketball and softball while getting my degree in early childhood education, but I knew from the beginning that I had no athletic future beyond college. There was no WNBA and no outlet beyond recreational leagues for women softball players. After graduation I found that, for the first time in my life, I had no competitive athletic outlet. Unless I joined a recreational league or found a pickup game at a local gym, my playing days were effectively over

Golf changed that. I saw the women at the club having a grand old time competing against each other. I saw them trying their best on the course, celebrating their victories, and agonizing over their losses, all while enjoying the company of their fellow golfers. Those were the things I missed when I hung up my cleats and put the basketballs away. Plus, I liked the clothes, the shoes, and the hats I saw on the golf course. This was the first sport I'd ever seen where the fashion was neat and, well, fashionable.

I decided to give the silly game a try. With $100 from the tips I'd made, I assembled a set of clubs out of the lost-and-found bin and set out mimicking the swings of the golfers I saw on the course. It never dawned on me that these people were not great or even good players and that copying their golf swings was a mistake. Fortunately, a kind pro named Ed Oldfield, one of the nation's finest instructors, took me under his wing.

"Hit it as far and as hard as you can," Ed told me during our first lesson together. I did as instructed, and the ball flew a decent distance.

"Again," he said. I did as I was told.

"Okay," Ed said after I had hit a dozen balls as hard as I could. "If you have the desire and the determination to work hard and learn this game, I'll coach you. If not, don't come back."

"But, Ed," I said. "I can't afford lessons. I'm a schoolteacher. I took the job as a cart girl because I'm one step away from poverty."

"Don't worry about that," he said. "If you want to learn, I'll teach you."

Not only did Ed teach me the fundamentals of the golf swing, he taught me how to play the game, how to conduct myself on the golf course, how to score, and how to win. I practiced on the driving range, the putting green, and the chipping area for two years before I ever played my first round of golf. Before school I was out hitting balls, and I'd slip out and roll a few putts during lunch. After school I was out at the course until dark. Ed would come by and offer tips and drills, and I'd go off and practice for a few more hours.

I did this, nonstop, for twenty-four months, and I loved every minute of it. My financial situation hadn't improved—I didn't play during that two-year period because I couldn't afford it—but I had a new challenge, a new athletic endeavor that I knew I would never outgrow, and I loved it. I had no aspirations of turning pro. It wasn't even a dream. I simply wanted to learn the game for me, for my own self-confidence, my own competitive needs, and my desire to be outdoors and in the company of fun, funny, like-minded people. Golf gave me all of that, and a lot more.

When I finally did play, I shot an 82 in my first round from the men's tees at the TPC of Scottsdale. Ed paid for my green fees. He also gave me a set of Pings he had in stock. But more than anything he gave me confidence in myself as a golfer and as a person.

I played with a couple of LPGA touring pros that first day, and they were stunned when we totaled the scores. You weren't supposed to break 90 your first time out. You weren't supposed to break 120 in your first round. I later learned that ninety-five percent of all golfers have never broken 100, and ninety percent of golfers who play regularly and who subscribe to at least one golf magazine have never broken 100. It was a good thing I didn't know those numbers at the time. I thought 82 was okay, but I wasn't satisfied with it. I could do better.

A year later I was playing, and winning, on the Players West Tour, a mini-tour for aspiring tour players. I had made it to the finals of LPGA qualifying in my first attempt, but having only played golf for one year, I lacked the experience to compete against the greatest women golfers in the world. After two years on the Players West Tour, I played a season on the Japanese LPGA Tour, then returned home where I played four years on the Futures Tour.

It wasn't always easy. I can't tell you the number of times I've sworn I was quitting golf forever. There have been days when I played so badly I wondered why I even bothered showing up. Surely there were better and more productive ways to spend four daylight hours than beating myself up while chasing a silly ball around. I could have been reading a book, getting some work done, or watching the news. Playing golf was the least productive and certainly the most maddening waste of a perfectly good afternoon I could have imagined.

You've probably been right there with me. You get so flustered by your ineptitude on the golf course that you wonder why you didn't stay home and plant petunias. This usually happens right after you've had one of your best rounds ever. Golf is like that. The game gives just enough to suck you in, to make you feel confident, even cocky with your rate of improvement. Then, in an instant, golf snatches it all away, leaving you twitching in a spastic heap.

A lot of women throw their hands up and say, "To heck with it."

While women represent the majority of new players entering the game each year, an equal number of women quit golf for good every year. They play a couple of times, get frustrated, and walk away. I know the feeling, and if you've played golf for any length of time, you know it too.

There is also the gender issue. No matter how empowered I felt on the basketball court or the softball field, in the classroom or on the ski slopes, I knew that I was competing against other women. There wasn't much gender-crossover in sports when I was growing up. Golf was the first sport I ever played where I could (and did) compete head-to-head against men on the same course, at the same time, and under the same rules and conditions. Just like all the women I've coached over the years, I was a little intimidated by that, especially in the beginning when I was trying to find my way in this new game. Then Ed gave me one of the greatest lessons I have ever received. He said, "The game doesn't care if you're a man or a woman. It doesn't care what you look like. It doesn't care how long you've been playing. All the game cares about are the numbers on the scorecard. In that respect, everybody who tees up a golf ball is equal."

I knew that if I worked harder than everyone else around me that I could post the best numbers. That knowledge gave me confidence to go ahead and take chances, to forge ahead even when I was getting sideways glances from men in my profession. It's a lesson I remember to this day.

What I didn't realize when I made the decision to play golf for a living was how tough the lifestyle would be. Traveling every week, living out of hotels and suitcases with no social life outside the ropes was a little more than I'd bargained for. I loved playing, but I disliked tour life. After seven years, I decided I should take my career in another direction. I had loved being a schoolteacher but hated the bureaucracy and stodginess of the system. I loved golf but disliked the travel and social isolation. Maybe there was a way to combine the good parts of both.

My first job as a golf instructor was at the TPC Golf Schools, where I worked alongside Jay Lumpkin, one of the gurus of the modern game. Watching him teach was like watching Mozart compose a symphony. It was another lesson that would serve me well as my career progressed.

As I started teaching others, I realized that my anxieties in golf weren't unique. Women who attended our schools tended to migrate to me, and I learned that we all shared the same phobias and fears. We were all scared of looking out of place; anxious about hitting a bad shot in front of a group of men; self-conscious about the amount of time we took on the course. All the silly fears I thought resulted from my own neurosis turned out to be par for the course.

That epiphany led to my current teaching style: a holistic approach to the game that not only helps women improve their shots and scores but gives them a sense of belonging, of making the game their own. If I can help a woman build confidence in herself by improving her golf game or make her a little more self-assured in a predominately male setting, then I've done more than teach golf: I've given someone a lesson in life.

A smile crossed my lips as I pondered the question before me. I would keep most of my thoughts to myself that day, just as I felt I had kept the game of golf for myself for more than a decade.

"More than anything, I love it," I told my interviewer. "I wake up every morning and I can't wait to get to the lesson tee to help my next pupil. Maybe it's just my nurturing nature or the fact that I always wanted to be a teacher. Whatever it is, I love what I do. I came to the game late in life; played golf competitively for seven years; and learned to teach from some of the greatest instructors in history. But above all, I do it because I can't imagine doing anything else."

I got the job that day. And every time I see a woman I've helped who has a smile on her face; every time someone says, "Cindy, I broke 90 today, and I didn't have a single three-putt green"; and every time I see someone's confidence grow with each ball struck in practice, I know that I made the right choice.

I found my way in golf because of the help and guidance of some wonderful, caring instructors. Now I'm a teacher. Hopefully, I can help you find your way in this game as well.

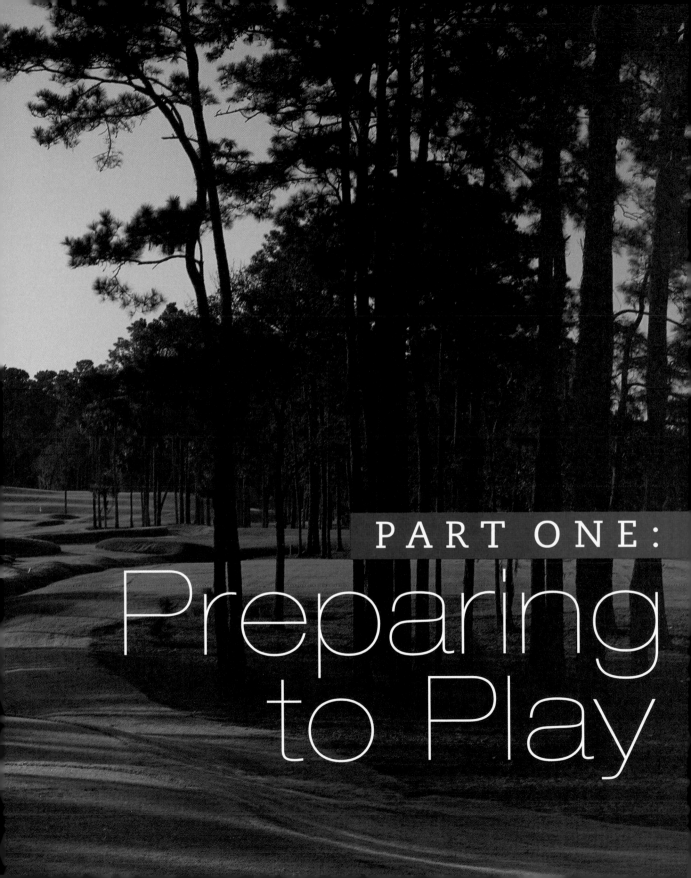

PART ONE:

Preparing to Play

I WAS GIVING A GOLF LESSON to a female business executive not long ago when, out of the blue, she said something that struck a chord with me. "You know, Cindy," she said, "I work with hundreds of men and women, and it still amazes me. You can say the same thing to a man and a woman and get two totally different interpretations of what was said. It's like we have two separate languages, one for each gender, but nobody will admit it."

At the time I made a joke, saying, "Well, at least woman-speak is more advanced." But the more I thought about it, the more I realized my student was onto something.

1 Learning How to Learn

It seems so obvious that it shouldn't need to be said, but it's so profound and so often overlooked it can't be said enough. Women and men are different. I know that isn't film-at-eleven news for anybody, but as my student pointed out, a lot of people ignore or forget that men and women process data differently. We communicate differently, analyze things differently, and speak, feel, listen, and learn in distinctly separate ways.

As I pondered this, I realized these differences apply to everything from physics to cooking to simple questions like "How does the pasta taste?" or "What does that feel like?"

Because I relate everything to golf and golf instruction, I started thinking about how these differences affect the way women and men learn to play the game. While most teachers acknowledge the physical differences between men and women, few, if any, modify their teaching to accommodate those differences, nor do they consider the possibility that women learn differently than men.

I see it all the time. A woman takes a lesson from a male instructor and the first thing the teacher tells her is to "fire" her hips through the downswing or to "release the club through impact by pronating and supinating the forearms." Can you imagine anything more useless? The best one I heard was a male instructor telling his petite female student to "Imagine you're swinging at a low, outside curveball." A low, outside curveball! This woman wouldn't have known which end of a baseball bat to hold, but that was the example her golf instructor used to communicate a particular feeling. If I'd been taught that way in the beginning I probably would have said, "To heck with it," and gone back to the ski slopes.

But I was lucky. I learned from the best in the business—both men and women—who understood the need to communicate and coach in a language and with methods that I understood.

As a woman, the golf instruction process probably intimidates you. I know it scared the wits out of me when I first started. Fortunately I had a great teacher, a mentor who had worked with great women professionals like Betsy King, Jan Stephenson, and Alice Miller and who understood the anxieties most women have when it comes to learning the game.

Why We Play

The first thing Ed Oldfield asked me when we stood on the lesson tee together for the first time was, "Why do you want to play golf?"

It seemed like a simple question, but I didn't have a good answer. "I'm not sure, Ed," I said. "I can't play basketball and softball the rest of my life, so I'm looking for a new game. I see all these people having a great time, they dress well, they obviously love it—I want to give it a go."

That sufficed because it was an honest answer. Too often, when I ask my students the same question, I get a blank stare or a curious shrug. Even women who have been playing golf for years can't tell me what they hope to accomplish by taking lessons. "What are your goals? What are you hoping to accomplish? Why are you here with me on the lesson tee?" are all questions I ask before I impart the first morsel of advice to one of my students. Unfortunately, I get a lot of I-don't-know-type answers.

Golf is an individual sport. There are thousands of variables in the game and millions of ways to learn. In order to reach your full potential as a golfer you have to find the method and the mechanics that work best for your body type and skill level. But before you can learn anything, you have to determine what kind of golfer you want to be. Are you taking lessons (and reading this book) because you like the outdoors and think spending four hours on a manicured golf course constitutes a well-spent afternoon? Are you learning to play for business? Do you want to win your club championship or Ladies' City Amateur title? Is it your husband or a friend you're trying to impress? Or do you simply want to occasionally win a chit in your Tuesday morning golf/social group? There is no right or wrong answer, but before you venture into any sort of game-improvement plan, you need to be honest with yourself. Answering the "Why am I doing this?" question before you get started makes the process a lot easier and a lot more fun.

The "Ah Ha" Moment

Unfortunately, golf isn't a paint-by-numbers sport. There is no step-one, -two, and -three to the process. It's not a cake we're baking where the recipe is written down, nor is it like following the assembly instructions in the Christmas box, even the ones an MIT mechanical engineer couldn't follow. You can't simply put peg "A" into peg hole "B" and become a good golfer.

Golf is not easy. It's not a game you or anyone else will ever master. That's a big part of why so many people love it. One day you will take a lesson or read a tip in a book or magazine and you'll say to yourself, "Voilà! I've got it." You will be convinced that you understand everything there is to know about the game and you're on your way to great scores. Then, two days later, you feel like you've never held a club in your life. Your shots go everywhere, your swing feels awful, and you can't find any motion that feels remotely comfortable. I'd love to tell you that this is a problem I can easily remedy, but it's not. It's just the way golf is.

What I can do is help you learn how to learn.

Have you ever taken a class where the material was so foreign to you that you had no idea what the instructor was saying? There are few things in the world more frustrating. I know; I've had my share of those experiences. You're listening, concentrating, hoping that something will eventually make sense, but nothing does. You wonder if you're alone in this quandary. Then you wonder if you're just plain dumb. Anxiety sets in and soon your head begins to throb.

Then, out of nowhere, your teacher says one thing, gives one example or makes one analogy, and everything clicks. You get it. It's like the blinders have been lifted and all the gobbledygook suddenly makes perfect sense. You lift your head and raise your eyebrows in amazement that what had seemed mind-numbing only moments before now looks perfectly logical and orderly, simple even.

I call this the "Ah Ha" moment, the moment the lightbulb flickers on and you see everything you couldn't see before. You want to stand up and scream, "Eureka!" when this happens, but you usually just sit back, cross your arms, and let a satisfied smile creep onto your face.

So, what causes these "Ah Ha" moments? Why is it that we can be bewildered by a concept one minute and see everything so clearly mere seconds later? The information hasn't changed. The concepts aren't any easier, and our IQs didn't magically inch up a few points while we were listening. So, what makes us understand now what we didn't get a minute ago?

The answer is in the delivery. Your teacher finally said or did something that your brain registered. It might have been a visual cue or a mental image or a technical explanation that finally made sense. The trigger, whatever it was, allowed your brain to process the information.

Golf instruction is no different than the classroom. I've seen students who have attended clinics or taken private lessons from less experienced instructors who walk away without learning a thing. The teacher might as well have been speaking Swahili.

I'm as guilty of this as anyone. There have been plenty of times I've been in the middle of the lesson, explaining everything I know about the nuances of the swing and loving the tenor of my own voice while I'm saying it, when I see a glazed blank mask falling over my student's face. At that point I know I've lost her.

Fortunately I've been teaching long enough to stop when I see my student's eyes cross. At that point I try a different route. I know that people absorb information about golf in different ways. If I fail to connect with a student—that is, if the student doesn't understand anything I'm saying—I know that the student processes information differently from the way I'm teaching, so I change methods.

There are four ways you process information about the golf swing. They are:

- *Visual*

- *Feel*

- *Technical*

- *Auditory*

Visual

Visual learning is just that—learning by seeing. Most of the students I've encountered learn to one degree or another through visuals. That's why video lessons have become so popular. If I can show a student what her golf swing looks like, she has a better chance of understanding what she needs to change and what she needs to work on to make her a better player.

Kids are great visual learners, because they mimic so well. You've probably heard the story of Tiger Woods, who before he was two, watched his father hit balls into a net in the family's garage. Young Tiger then crawled down from his highchair, grabbed his plastic club, and made a perfect golf swing. It sounds unreal, but I've seen it more than once. Young children absorb visual information much better than hardwired adults. They can mimic almost anything. That's why when I'm giving a lesson to a junior I hit more balls than I do when I'm teaching an adult. I want the junior to see and copy the proper technique.

Most of us lose a little of that kidlike knack for imitation as we grow older, but visual learning is still the number-one way golfers learn. Korean superstar Mi Hyun Kim, who won Rookie of the Year honors on the LPGA Tour and racked up three wins in her first two years on tour, said she watched John Daly when she was young and decided she wanted to hit the ball like John. If you see Mi Hyun's swing today you'll see she was successful. Her long, loose backswing is unconventional, but it's almost identical to the grip-it-and-rip-it swing John Daly has been using for years.

Another Korean star, Se Ri Pak, studies videos of her swing from all angles as part of her game-improvement regimen. She, too, is a visual learner.

The problem with visual learning is few people recognize how much information they process visually. Witnesses to crimes often say things like, "I didn't get a good look at him. I'm not sure I can describe what I saw." But when investigators methodically walk the witness through the process, taking step-by-step notes, the results are stunning. Sketch artists have come up with incredible likenesses of criminals because of the recollections of witnesses who "didn't get a good look."

▶
Full-length mirrors are a must for visual learning.

I see the same thing with many of my female students on the lesson tee. I'll say things like, "Can you see how your hands are working too much on the takeaway?" and the student will answer, "Oh, I really can't learn much by looking. I'm a feel player." When I probe a little further, I find that the golfer in question is not a feel player at all, but someone who learns by watching without realizing it.

Recently I taught a woman who had a terrible problem with laying the club off on the backswing. She rotated her hands on the takeaway in such a fashion that the club could never get high enough to make a good swing. She looked like she was swinging a baseball bat. Despite her insistence that she was a feel player, when I asked her about this swing flaw she said, "I just can't feel it." So, I broke out the camera and showed her a video of her swing. "Oh," she said. "I had no idea that was what I was doing." Within minutes she fixed her backswing.

This is just one example. I've seen it hundreds of times. People assume that because they can differentiate good shots from bad shots through feel that they are feel players when, in fact, they learn better through visuals.

Golfers of all ages and skill levels use visual aids to improve their games. How many times have you seen a golfer taking mock practice swings in front of a full-length mirror? I notice it almost every time I'm in a store where plenty of mirrors are available. If no one else is doing it, I usually take a few clubless practice swings of my own.

There's a good chance that you can learn a great deal about golf from visual aids. If you find yourself wondering what you look like with a club in your hands, or if you watch pros on television on the weekend and find yourself trying to mimic certain moves or positions, you are, at least in part, a visual learner.

Feel

Of course some players couldn't care less what they look like on video. I remember Hubert Green, the noted Senior PGA Tour player, saying that he watched a video of his swing once in his life and he almost threw up, so he never did it again.

Nancy Lopez is another player who doesn't take much stock in how her swing looks, and it's hard to argue with her success. Lopez learned the game from her father, and according to Nancy, the lessons she learned on the fundamentals of the swing were, "Bring the club up real slow; bring it up real high; extend your arms real far; hit the ball right on the sweet spot; and send it into the middle of the fairway." Simple advice, but it worked. Nancy won forty-eight professional events and is in the LPGA Hall of Fame.

Both Hubert Green and Nancy Lopez are *feel* players, players who don't take much stock in finding the perfect, classic swing. They feel what works for them, and they work on that feeling.

A lot of teachers give their pupils analogies of what something should feel like, but that often tells you more about the teacher than the pupil. If a teacher says something like, "You need to feel like you're cracking a whip with your right hand as you bring the club down," that tells you the teacher has created a mental image of himself cracking a whip. It's what the teacher feels and what the teacher uses as a mental cue. The student might not have any idea what a bullwhip looks like.

Feel players are tougher to teach, because feelings are so subjective. One of the funniest stories from the golf instruction world is an old tale Bob Toski tells on himself. Toski, an excellent tour player in his day and one of the most respected instructors in the world for decades after he retired from competition, was teaching a student who simply couldn't grasp what Toski was saying. "I can't feel it. I can't feel it," the student kept saying. Finally, in utter frustration, Toski leaned over and bit the student on the forearm. "There," he said, "can you feel that?"

The best teachers, the ones who understand that their students are feel players, design drills and exercises that give the student the feelings they need for a good golf swing. I have a bag full of swing training aids—everything from a weighted club to a club with an extra-long shaft that swats you in the side if you swing it the wrong way—all designed to give players the feel of making a good golf swing.

If you're more interested in how something should feel instead of how it should look, then your brain probably responds better to feel than to visual input. And if that's the case, you need to find a teacher who understands your needs and who will give you the drills and teaching aids you need in order to improve.

Technical

Other people can't do anything until they know why. If they swing at a golf ball and it rolls down the fairway, they want to know the physics of what caused the ball to roll the way it did. If the ball slices they have to know the exact causes of that ball flight, from where the club was at impact to what path the club took to get into that position, to what the body was doing to get the club there in the first place.

Hall of Fame running back Marcus Allen is one of those. Marcus has been one of my students for years, so I understand how he processes information. If a ball slices, he wants to know why. What combination of factors contributed to the curvature of the ball during flight? What physical laws were in play? What swing mechanics led to that result? There are times when I've said, "Jeez, Marcus, I have no idea how this watch works, but I can tell you what time it is. Do you have to know everything? Can't you just take my word for it every now and then?"

The answer to that is always, "No." Marcus, like a lot of other golfers, is a technician. Before he can correct a problem, he has to fully understand it. It's an admirable trait, one that usually denotes a strong analytical mind, but Marcus and people like him tend to overanalyze their golf games.

You've seen them. They're the people who go through the mental checklist every time they hit a shot. (1) Light grip. (2) Left arm straight. (3) Head down. (4) Chin up. (5) Rear end out. (6) Right arm tucked. (7) Okay, now relax and make a great swing. It never quite works out the way they've planned, but you can't fault their thoroughness.

There are plenty of great players who are technical thinkers. Karrie Webb analyzes her swing mechanics and ball flight with the diligence and efficiency of a surgeon. She also won twenty-six professional titles, including a career Grand Slam (all four major championships) before her twenty-seventh birthday. It's hard to argue with that kind of success.

If you feel the need to know "why" in golf as much or more than the "what" or the "how to," then you might be a technical learner. There's nothing wrong with that. It's just something you should know before embarking on a campaign to become a better golfer.

You need a teacher who can communicate the basics of the golf swing in logical, progressive steps. If you get someone who tells you how the swing should look or how it should feel without first explaining the laws and principles that make it work, you've picked the wrong teacher.

Auditory

Auditory learners are rare, but they also learn faster than the rest of us. People who respond to audio feedback tend to make physical adjustments quicker than those who have to see, feel, or analyze their situation. Why do you think football and basketball coaches carry whistles? It's not because they don't like to yell. They've learned over the years that audio conditioning gets results faster than other stimuli.

Auditory response is one of the most basic of human instincts. If you hear a baby cry, you instinctively react. If an alarm goes off, you stop what you're doing and turn your attention toward the sound. If a coach has trained you to stop or start on the sound of a whistle, you react when you hear that whistle blow. Studies show that behavior modification occurs forty percent faster when stimulated with auditory feedback. That's why a gun goes off to start the 100-meter dash instead of a green light flashing or a flag dropping. Runners get out of the gate quicker on the sound of a gun.

Golfers can have similar reactions. The sound of a good crisp iron shot, for example, provides instant feedback. You know you've hit a good shot before your eyes ever find the ball. Likewise, the thud or thwack of a poorly hit shot sends chills up your spine. I've had students turn away in disgust after hearing the clunk of a poor shot and never see their balls roll onto the green and into the hole. They knew they didn't hit the ball well, so the results were irrelevant.

I've seen and used several different audio training tools as part of my teaching. One that is particularly effective is a windmill on the end of a golf club that gives a distinct "swish" sound at the point of impact.

▲

The windmill club gives instant auditory feedback, and students improve faster when they use it.

If a student is swinging the club faster at the top of the swing than at the impact position, the swish won't happen. The only time you hear the sound is when you've released the golf club at the right spot in the swing. This is a great tool for audio-sensitive learners. All I have to do is say, "Swing until you hear the swish." And it works! Auditory learners improve quicker by using this simple teaching aid than they would if I stood on the range and talked to them all afternoon.

Another less popular but equally effective tool is the beeping shoe insole. This tool fits into the insole of your shoe and is pressure sensitive. It has an antenna and a monitor (similar to a baby monitor). You program the monitor to set off an alarm when a certain percentage of your body weight is on a particular foot. So if I have a student who isn't getting on her left side quickly or fully enough, I simply set the monitor to beep when seventy to seventy-five percent of her weight is applied to the insole. Then I say, "Shift your weight until you hear the beep." It's amazing how quickly students respond.

Why Is This Important?

So why is it important to know what kind of learner you are? When I was playing golf not long ago at the TPC at Sawgrass I saw a man and his wife a hole ahead of me. But I heard them as if they were sitting in the golf cart with me.

"Why in the world can't you do it?" the man said. "Your club is dropping way below parallel at the top of your backswing. It looks terrible!"

The woman, obviously having gotten this little tip before, said, "I can't feel it, and I don't care what it looks like. I just hit it farther than you, so why don't you try a backswing like mine."

"You'll never be consistent," he insisted. "As long as your swing looks like that, you'll hit it good one minute and bad the next."

"When I start hitting it worse than you, you can criticize," she said. "Right now, it feels fine, and I'm sticking with it."

"Stubborn," he said.

"Jackass," she said.

I'm glad I was behind that group and not playing in their foursome. The problem with this couple—in addition to both of them being strong-willed personalities—was that the man was telling his wife what her swing "looked" like and she was telling him how it "felt." They might have gotten along well in every other aspect of life, but because of the different ways each of them learned, they were never going to get along on the golf course.

Picking an Instructor

No matter what your skill level, you need to find a golf instructor you trust and understand, and one who improves your game. Golf instruction comes from numerous sources (including the book you're now reading). As a woman, I doubt you'll ever play or practice golf around men when you aren't offered at least one tip. Family and friends are the worst at this. If I hear one more husband tell his wife to keep her head down, I think I'll scream. All these pseudo-teachers are well meaning, but the majority of them don't have the technical expertise or communication skills to be effective golf instructors. For that you need a professional.

Too many women I know are intimidated by the prospect of learning golf, so they take the easy route. They go to the local recreation center and sign up for a group clinic from some guy they've never heard of whose credentials aren't available. Or they go to their local golf course or driving range and ask something like, "Do you have anyone here who gives lessons?" When a young kid who looks like the boy who bagged your groceries last week says, "Sure," these impressionable women sign up for a lesson without further delay.

Nothing could be worse for your game. Golf instructors are like any other working professionals; if they're worth their salt, they won't mind you asking a few questions. Among the things you need to ask any teachers you're considering are:

1. How long have you been teaching?

2. How many lessons do you give in a day, a week, a month, or a year?

3. What is your experience outside this course or club?

4. How many women do you teach?

5. What success stories can you tell me about your other students?

6. Tell me about your philosophy of teaching.

7. What would be the first thing you would do with me if I became your student?

8. Do you use video?

9. What other training tools do you use when teaching?

10. Can you provide a list of references?

You might want to probe deeper, but these are the must-ask questions you should put to any golf instructor. If the pro is put off by these questions, he or she isn't worth hiring.

You are the client. You wouldn't hire a housekeeper, a gardener, an accountant, a lawyer, and you certainly wouldn't let a surgeon operate on you without asking a few questions. You shouldn't let your golf pro get off any easier.

Free Advice Is Worth Exactly What You Pay for It

In pondering how to broach the subject of husbands, boyfriends, and other companions and acquaintances offering free advice on the golf course, I decided to ask a group of experts. During one of my weekly women's golf clinics, I asked: "What should I say in my book about husbands giving golf advice to their wives?" The responses ranged from "Tell them to shut up and mind their own business," to "Unless they want our advice on how to fix the sink or change the oil in the car, tell them to keep their opinions to themselves."

This went on for a couple of minutes with laughter after each biting comeback. In the end, the most sanguine advice from my group was: "Women should smile, nod, say, 'Yes, dear,' and completely ignore them."

Men feel compelled to give women advice about golf. It's in their genes, like hunting, gathering, and clicking the television remote. Unless your husband, boyfriend, or male playing partner is also your teaching pro, the best advice is to ignore any free advice. Free advice is worth exactly what you pay for it. You should always be polite, even when the advice you're getting is something as silly as, "You're looking up!" or "You're not throwing the clubhead through the ball enough!" Just smile, nod, and ignore it.

Your golf swing is between you and your instructor. Part of making the game your own is taking command of the advice you will and will not accept. You should never be stubborn or rude. But you should take charge of your game. Once you do, you'll have a lot more fun on the course.

Managing Expectations

Once you've hired a teacher, the next conversation you need to have is on the subject of expectations. Both you and your instructor have to be reasonable in terms of how good you want to be and how much work you plan to put into your golf game.

I can't tell you the number of times I've been snookered by a student with unrealistic expectations. She will invariably tell me how desperately she wants to improve and how she's willing to do whatever it takes to get better. So I work with her, getting her to make better swings, then I prescribe a number of drills, some exercises, and a reasonable practice regimen to train the body on the new moves. A couple of weeks later I see this student again and she is swinging the same way she did before our first lesson. "Did you practice what we went over last time?" I ask.

"Well, I didn't get out to the practice tee as much as I would have liked," she answers.

"How about the drills? Did you do what we discussed?"

"Well . . . not really."

"Any exercises?"

"No."

Yet she wonders why she's making the same abysmal swings and hitting the same poor shots she did the last time we had a lesson.

Golf takes practice. Good golf takes lots of practice, and great golf requires more hard work than most people are willing to accept. Before you become too immersed in your newfound love for the game, you need to sit down with your instructor and map out a reasonable strategy for practicing and playing that includes all the distractions you have in your life.

Most of us don't have two hours a day to hit balls, but that's okay. If you're realistic about what you can and can't do in terms of practicing, playing, exercising, and drilling, you won't fall victim to false expectations. And you're less likely to become frustrated when the game doesn't come to you in a snap.

Keeping It Fun

Anyone who tells you that you can lay off this game for a couple of years, head out to the first tee, and have a wonderful experience has either never played the game or is intentionally trying to deceive you. There's no more anxious feeling in the world than standing on that first tee and wondering who's going to see you make a fool of yourself. And there's no more frustrating feeling than spending all afternoon on the course without hitting at least one or two good shots.

That's why I suggest that when my students are working on swing changes or making certain setup adjustments that they forget about playing by the rules for a while. Don't keep score when you're trying to learn something new, and don't worry if you hit an errant shot into the bushes. Drop another ball, forget about the one you lost, and play on. If you feel you've been on a hole too long, pick up and go to the next tee. If you're tired, quit. You aren't competing in the U.S. Women's Open, and if you're worried that your friends might snicker at your inability to finish a round, you need to reevaluate your friends.

Golf isn't easy, but it shouldn't be torture either. Enter it with a good attitude, and you'll never grow tired of learning.

I RECENTLY SPENT A WEEKEND teaching and playing golf with the CEO of an old established New York firm (a company whose name you would recognize), who also happened to be a woman. She had flown in from New York on Friday afternoon; we'd spent a few hours on the range on Saturday morning; and Saturday afternoon we had a tee time on the Stadium Course at the TPC at Sawgrass. After lunch we loosened up, and trotted over to the first tee when the starter called our names.

2 Making the Game Your Own

- -

We had to wait a couple of minutes for the group ahead of us to clear the fairway. When they moved out of our way, my student and I hit our tee shots, got in the cart, and drove off.

Seconds later a foursome of men pulled up behind us. "Oh dear," my student said. "Maybe I should pick my ball up and ride this hole. I don't want to hold up those men behind us."

I couldn't believe what I was hearing! "What are you talking about?" I said, somewhat incredulously.

"Those men," she said, pointing to the group of gentlemen behind us. "I don't want to hold them up."

- -

"You aren't holding anybody up," I said. "There's a group directly in front of us. You paid to be here just like everybody else. Relax and enjoy your day. As long as we keep up with the group ahead of us and don't vandalize the golf course, we have just as many rights out here as anybody."

This shouldn't have been a revolutionary concept to this woman. She manages a business with millions of dollars in revenues, and she has hundreds of male employees working for her. If anybody should have been gender neutral, it was this student. But alas, she proved to be like most women on the golf course: intimidated, anxious, and willing to subjugate her own game and good time to any man on the premises.

If you learn nothing else from this book, you need to know that *you belong* on the golf course as much or more than any other man, woman, or child who pokes a tee in the ground. Your skill level and gender should have no bearing on your commitment to golf or to your enjoyment of the game.

For too long women were relegated to back-of-the-bus status when it came to our game. We could only play on Tuesday mornings or late Sunday afternoons. We weren't allowed in the clubhouse (a policy that's still in effect in some places) and we couldn't be members. Now women are an integral part of the golf landscape in America. We represent the largest segment of new players entering the game each year, and many women now serve on the boards of some of the most prestigious golf clubs in the world. In the 1990s Judy Bell became the first woman ever elected president of the United States Golf Association, and during that same period Judy Rankin became the first female golf commentator to successfully transition her broadcast skills to the men's tour. Today everyone from Barbara Bush to Madonna plays golf. It has become the chic sport for today's woman.

Any holdover feelings of inferiority women might bring with them to the first tee should be dunked into the nearest water hazard. This is our game. We should feel comfortable and confident every time we pull into the parking lot at the club or step onto the tee. Golf isn't, in and of itself, empowering. But the confidence you gain, the skills you develop, the relationships you cultivate, and the lessons you learn on the golf course are unmatched. You should enjoy your time with the game. You will become a better person because of it.

Family Affair

One of golf's great traditions is a love for the game passed down through generations from parents to children. Judy Rankin took up the game at age six when her father carted her to the course. Judy followed that same family tradition by exposing her son, Tuey, to golf when he was old enough to walk and carry a club. Nancy Lopez tells a great story about her entrée into the game. "I used to love to tag along with my father and mother when they played on a municipal course in Roswell, New Mexico," Lopez says. "Dad was a pretty good player, and my mother made up in enthusiasm what she lacked in skill. I think she enjoyed being out in the fresh air with Dad and me as much as anything else. One day, when I was eight years old, Dad took a 4-wood out of Mom's bag, handed me a tee and a ball, and told me to hit it, and hit it again, until I reached the green. From that moment on I was hooked, and they were hooked on me being hooked."

Golf is full of wonderful stories like Nancy's: fathers playing with daughters, mothers playing with sons, families building a bond around golf and building traditions that last a lifetime. One of the best family golf stories involves former LPGA Rookie of the Year and current ESPN golf commentator Laura Baugh. When Laura was growing up in Cocoa Beach, Florida, her father would take her and her two brothers to the course every day. "Father devised a game for us he called 'The codfish tournament,'" Laura recalls. "This was loosely based on the game the Lost Boys played in Never-Never Land with Peter Pan. I would play the forward tees, my brothers would play the middle tees, and my dad would play the back tees. Sometimes we would play three-hole matches, sometimes nine-hole matches, and sometimes they went on all day. At the end, the loser had to stand up at the dinner table and say: 'I am a codfish.' It was a fate worse than death for a little girl, so I would play as hard as I could." Today, Laura continues the tradition with her children, E.J., Haley, and Robbie, all promising young golfers who play with their mom in Orlando. "It's a family tradition," Laura says. "Hopefully they'll pass it on to their kids."

The list goes on and on. Karrie Webb credits her grandfather with introducing her to the game, and her parents continue to be her biggest supporters and fans. Tiger Woods's father wrote a book about his experiences raising a young golf prodigy, and Kultida Woods, Tiger's mother, can be found in the gallery at every major championship. My friend Johnny Miller introduced his boys to the game, and they have become successful players in their own rights, and Charlie and Debbie Howell, proud parents of Charles Howell III, are rarely absent when their son plays.

Debbie Howell and Kultida Woods don't play that well, and Karrie's mom isn't a world-beater either. But these mothers found a different motivation for going to the course every day. Their children were their top priorities, and golf was a family affair. The dividends these parents earned for their efforts are undeniable. The paybacks you'll receive are just as rich. Golf can be an instrument for bringing a family together. And it is a game where traditions can be passed down through generations.

Friends and Relations

At various spots in these pages I mention some of my more famous clients and friends, celebrities of sorts as well as business executives and sports figures whom I've met throughout my many journeys in the game. I don't talk about friends like Vijay Singh, Marcus Allen, Charles Barkley, Rick Berry, Tom Brokaw, or Matt Lauer because I love name-dropping—in fact I hate it!—I do it to make the point that golf opens doors and provides you with introductions and opportunities you might never otherwise see. What are the chances of a girl from New Jersey who grew up playing softball and beating her older brothers on the basketball court becoming friends with the likes of a former U.S. Open champion, a British Open winner, a guy with a green jacket from Augusta National in his closet, as well as world-renowned journalists, executives, and a couple of Super Bowl MVPs? Golf opened those doors for me, as well as many others.

I've visited five continents because of golf, meeting people and seeing things I could only have dreamed about had it not been for this game. In the summer of 2001, I was asked to go to China to give a series of clinics. Talk about a cultural experience! Golf is new in China. They have more than 2 billion people and only six golf courses, all built within the last ten years. But as with most endeavors, the Chinese people have embraced golf with more enthusiasm than I've seen from any other group. They work harder, learn quicker, and embrace the discipline of the game with more fervor than do Americans, Europeans, or even other Asians. I was surprised by the enthusiastic response I received in China and thrilled by the embrace my audience gave the game. I felt like Marco Polo! I keep tabs on a lot of the best players in China, and I have become a great friend to some of the leaders from that nation. None of this would have been possible were I not involved in golf. The game opened this door, like it has opened countless others in my life.

It can open just as many doors for you.

Equipment

I met a woman not long ago who booked a golf lesson with me in Florida. She was an intermediate player who wanted to improve enough to be competitive in her local club championship and enjoy herself more when she and her husband traveled to fine resort courses around the world. I was impressed by her knowledge, her realistic expectations, and by the fact that she had established some obtainable goals. But before we ventured out of the clubhouse for the lesson tee, she asked a question that threw me for a loop.

"So, Cindy," she said, "what kind of clubs do you think I should be playing?"

I hesitated for a moment before saying, "I don't know."

"Well," she said, "since I'm going to be working harder on my game in the next year or so I thought you could recommend something."

"I'm sorry," I said. "I'll be happy to recommend clubs after a couple of lessons, but before I see you swing, I can't. It would be like a doctor telling you what pills you should take before examining you. I can't just look at a person and make a recommendation."

Neither can your local pro or golf-store owner, and anyone who says they can is trying to rip you off.

Other than yachting, I can't think of a single sport where you can spend money as fast as you can in golf. Balls alone range from $2 to $5 apiece. Clubs can run anywhere from $100 for a used set from the lost-and-found bin (like my first set) to $500 a club for the latest and greatest titanium marvels. Retooling your equipment can get a little pricey. That's why I tell all my students to view golf equipment as an investment, and to take charge of their own games. Club salesmen can be like car salesmen: They can see a woman coming from a mile away. You are responsible for taking charge of your game. That starts by taking control of your equipment.

If you were investing in a stock, bond, mutual fund, or commodity, you wouldn't simply pick the most expensive items and assume they were the best. Hopefully you would do your homework. You would examine the performance of each product you were considering, and you would weigh that performance against your personal investment goals. You would balance the risks against the potential rewards and look at how each particular vehicle fits into your overall strategy. That's what smart investors do.

Golf purchases should be examined with the same scrutiny. Before you buy into the hype about the latest performance-enhancing technological gadgetry and how it's guaranteed to shave five shots off your scores, you have to have a strategy, a plan of action for finding the right equipment for your needs. Some rules you should keep in mind whenever you're considering an equipment change are:

- *There are no self-hitters.* The greatest golf club in the world is only as good as the person swinging it. If you're looking to buy a game, you might want to consider bingo. Equipment can help you. Quality equipment that fits your body and your swing will help you hit the ball farther and straighter. But it won't do the work for you.

- *Don't take just anybody's word for it.* I recently gave a lesson to an eleven-year-old girl who had more natural talent than anyone I'd ever seen at that age. It was stunning how naturally she swung the club and how far and straight she hit every shot. I was also amazed when I saw the kind of irons she was playing.

"Who put you in those clubs?" I asked.

"I bought them from a guy who said they were what I needed," she said.

"Did this 'guy' watch you swing?" I asked.

"No, he just said that given my age and size, these were the clubs I needed."

They weren't at all what she needed, but the poor kid had no idea. She was taking the advice of a seemingly knowledgeable adult who let her down. "You need to be swinging blades with steel shafts that are tipped stiff," I told her. "Your swing speed and angle of attack are such that blades will perform for you, plus, you'll be able to spin the ball better and get better feedback from solid shots."

This was exactly the advice this little girl needed. And exactly what she hadn't gotten from pros who were more interested in selling a set of clubs they had in stock than in fitting a talented young golfer into the clubs she needed.

■   *All women do not need graphite-shafted clubs.* It's one of those lingering myths, the kind that takes on a life of its own no matter how often or how vigorously you attempt to dispel it. If I've heard it once I've heard it a thousand times: Women need graphite shafts in all their clubs.

That's bunk. And if you're one of the millions of golfers who bought into this nonsense, you need to forget you ever heard it. Women need graphite shafts like a fish needs a bicycle. Clubhead speed, swing arc, clubface angle at impact, and hand and arm strength are all variables in determining what kind of shafts you need. Gender has nothing to do with it.

The biggest difference between graphite and steel shafts is the weight. If you made a graphite shaft the same overall weight as a steel shaft it would be so strong you could hang it in the gym and do chin-ups on it. Because graphite is lighter, a lot of so-called golf experts say that the weaker sex should automatically be swinging graphite shafts. That logic is as offensive as it is wrongheaded.

I have graphite shafts in my driver and 3-wood, and steel shafts in every other club in my bag. That combination fits my game perfectly. Until I see you swing, I can't tell you what combination of graphite and steel is right for you. Neither can a shop clerk who has never seen you hit a ball. Don't be fooled into believing otherwise.

■   *Looks do matter.* Ugly golf clubs might perform well in laboratory testing, but if you can't get comfortable looking at it when you set it down behind your ball, forget it. You're not going to hit a club well if you don't like the way it looks. You have to be able to line up a club toward your target, and feel comfortable that the club is going to perform for you. Looks play a role in that. No matter how great a new

club might claim to be, if you don't like the looks of it, move on to something else.

■ *Ladies' balls are repackaged rejects.* I had the opportunity to tour a golf ball plant recently, and I was stunned by what I saw. It turns out that all the balls coming through the assembly line were supposed to come out with the same compression—100+, the balls tour players use. But the assembly process isn't that precise, and a fair number of balls don't quite reach the maximum tolerances. So, what do some ball manufacturers do with these rejects? They cleverly repackage them as "ladies'" balls.

Don't fall prey to this gimmick. Hit a 100-compression golf ball. They are the ones the ball manufacturer was trying to make in the first place, and I challenge anyone in a blind test to accurately pick out a 100-compression ball from a "ladies'" ball.

Forget the hype. Hit only the best.

It's almost impossible for me to give you much generic advice on picking golf clubs since so much of the process is unique to you and your swing. But there are some general rules I recommend to all my students.

■ *If possible, choose a face-balanced putter.* Putters are one of the most subjective and personal items you can purchase. Some people love small, thin-bladed putters, while others want mallets the size of their feet. It's not up to me or anyone else to tell someone what kind of putter is right or wrong. My only recommendation is that you consider a "face-balanced" putter, that is, a putter that balances squarely with the clubface pointing to the sky when you perch it on your finger or lay it across a counter. Tests have shown that it's easier to keep the face of these putters square throughout the stroke, which is a key to making more putts. Other than that, I leave my students on their own when it comes to choosing a putter.

▲

Good wedges are a critical component for a good game.

■ *Don't skimp on your wedges.* I carry three wedges of varying lofts in my bag. This is the standard configuration for most pros these days. Some even carry four wedges, depending on the course they're playing. These wedges range in loft from 51- to 60-degrees with flanges that get progressively bigger as the lofts increase.

I recommend most of my intermediate to advanced students carry three wedges. Given the way courses are set up today, and with the majority of the shots you play coming within 100 yards of the hole, it's important that you come to the course with a complete complement of wedges for every conceivable shot.

■ *Err on the side of shorter clubs.* The number of experienced women golfers who continue to play with their husbands' hand-me-down clubs stuns me. For starters, these women have been in the game long enough to purchase their own golf clubs. But more important, their games suffer because the clubs they're playing are too long, too heavy, and the shafts are too stiff for their swings.

A lot of women fear they might sacrifice distance if they go with shorter clubs, but exactly the opposite is true. Shorter clubs are easier to control, which means you're going to make solid contact with the

The Beginner's Guide to Getting Started

If you've never played golf or if you're at the very early stages of the learning process, you're probably a little anxious or even a little scared. That's natural and understandable. Golf isn't a game where you can disappear in the crowd or fake your way through. When you stand on the first tee to hit your first shot, you are the center of the world. All eyes are on you, and your performance is being judged by the people in your group and by anyone else who happens to be standing nearby.

I know the feeling. There were plenty of times in my early years in golf when I wanted to walk off the course and throw my clubs in a Dumpster on the way to my car. But I knew that if I worked at golf, it could become something personal for me; a game no one else could control and no one could take away from me; something I could enjoy for the rest of my life.

You can enjoy it too, and at a reasonable cost. If you're just taking up the game, you should plan on spending a few hundred dollars to get outfitted. Beginning golfers don't need any more than six or seven clubs, which can be purchased piecemeal from a local golf shop. Used clubs are also a good option. Most shops have various used clubs either on display in a barrel or bin, or in the back room collecting dust. I recommend you assemble a set that includes:

1. A face-balanced putter
2. A sand wedge
3. A pitching wedge
4. A 7-iron
5. A 5-iron
6. A 3-wood

Don't spend a fortune on clothes either. You can play golf in sneakers. I did it for two years, and for a while that's exactly what you should do. You can also play in a casual but nice top and a pair of tasteful shorts or slacks. There's no reason to spend a fortune getting outfitted for a game you've never played and one you don't know if you're even going to like.

Plus, spending money on all the accoutrements of the game puts added pressure on you to do well. You say to yourself, "I've got to get better and get out on the course soon to justify all this money I spent on clothes and shoes." Because of this pressure you try too hard, and you let the natural frustrations of learning get to you. It's a vicious cycle, and one that can be avoided by adopting a prudent investment strategy while learning to play.

ball more often. Solid, straight, controlled shots go farther, as a rule, than off-center, off-line hits with longer clubs. If you have a choice between one inch over, and one inch under standard length, always err on the shorter side.

Good Players Should Be Fitted

When I was skiing competitively, I remember making the jump from stock equipment to custom-fitted skis, boots, and poles. It was a thrill, but it was also a necessity. As my skills and times improved, so did my need for more precision equipment that fit my body and my style of skiing.

Golf is no different. When I started out, a $100 set of clubs from the lost-and-found bin worked fine. As I improved I went to a standard set of Pings, a much more professional set of clubs. Now I have my clubs custom fit to my precise specifications. Loft, lie angle, shaft flex and flex point, and grip size are all variables I specifically check before any club goes into my bag.

Its hard to know when your skill level reaches the point where customizing clubs is worth the additional time and expense, but I usually establish a single-digit handicap as my barometer. Once your handicap falls below a 10, you should consider being professionally evaluated and custom fit for equipment.

Beware the Golf Diva!

I know some women who view golf as little more than an outdoor cocktail party. If you've been around the golf course much you've seen them, the social butterflies who dress to the nines for a day on the course and who never forget the Bloody Mary mix. They flit back and forth between members of their group, chatting and laughing, becoming more demonstrative with each passing hole, completely oblivious to the other people on the course.

Socializing while playing golf is fine, but you shouldn't fall into the "Golf Diva" trap of thinking the game is one big party. Some people take golf seriously. Having party girls playing in front of or behind them is offensive.

Golf is supposed to be fun, but it's no different than any other activity. Showing respect for those around you is the first rule. And if you play by that rule, you will never have a miserable day on the golf course.

ONE OF THE FIRST THINGS I ASK each of my students is, "What do you hope to accomplish? What are you trying to gain by taking this golf lesson?" The responses vary, but as I press the issue a recurring theme always pops up. "I want to get consistent," is the standard response. Sometimes "longer" is thrown in as a goal, as is "hitting the ball more solidly," but when I probe a little deeper, consistency always comes out as the one thing every golfer wants to obtain.

My response isn't always popular. "If you want to become consistent," I say, "you need to practice eight to ten hours a day, six days a week, for at least a year. Then and only then can you consistently hit good golf shots a majority of the time." My students are crestfallen when I break this news, but I feel like it's best not to soft sell the realities of the game. Golf is a difficult game.

3 Practice

There will be days when you feel invincible, when the swing seems so simple and easy that you wonder how on earth you could have struggled so long to master it. The next day you might feel like an uncoordinated geek who doesn't know which end of the club to hold. That's just the nature of the game.

Even the best in the world never reach nirvana when it comes to golf. Ben Hogan, universally recognized as one of the greatest ball strikers in history, said he never played a shot in a round that he hadn't hit at least a hundred times in practice. He also said he felt fortunate if he hit three shots a round exactly as he had intended. Players like Lori Kane and Se Ri Pak, two of the best ball strikers in women's golf, say the best they can hope for in any round is to manage their misses, keeping mistakes to a minimum by missing their shots in spots that aren't too bad. I have the good fortune of spending a lot of time with Vijay Singh, the man recognized as the most ardent practice fanatic on tour. But even Vijay, who practices from dawn till dusk more days than anyone in the world, admits that he'll never gain complete consistency in his game.

Before you read the next page; before you learn the first fundamental of the game; before you buy your next golf club, ball, or bag; or before you book your next tee time; you should commit to a practice schedule that is realistic and consistent with your goals.

One of my junior students came to me recently with the lofty goals I often hear from youngsters. "I want to play the tour," she said with great confidence.

"Good," I said. "How much do you practice?"

"At least a couple of hours a day, plus I play every day."

"Okay," I said. "You need to triple your practice time."

Her eyes grew to the size of saucers.

"If you don't practice six to eight hours a day, you're losing ground, and you don't have what it takes to make it as a professional," I said. "When I was playing for a living, I used to stand on the range and wait for the sun to come up so I could see to hit my first practice ball, and I would still be practicing that night when it was too dark to see. I once hit so many balls that I cracked two of my ribs. If you want to play the tour, that's the kind of commitment you have to make."

I didn't say this to discourage my student. I just wanted her to know the facts ahead of time. When I first took up golf, I practiced every day for two years before playing my first round of golf. During that time I spent hours working on drills that seemed to serve no useful purpose other than to make me look silly out on the range. These included things like hitting hundreds of balls with various plastic gadgets attached to my club to condition my body to the proper path and plane of the swing; taking half and quarter swings to hit punch shots; beating countless balls from severe downhill lies to improve my weight transfer and get the club on the proper plane on the downswing; and hitting balls off a board with tape on the face to determine where and how the clubhead was coming through impact. I know I must have looked like the oddest duck on the pond, out on the range every day with this or that gizmo, drilling on one or two moves that looked to the outsider as if they had little or no bearing on the swing. But I knew from my previous sports experiences that learning the correct technique on the front end paid immeasurable dividends later on.

Did I master the game? Of course not. I'm still working on the same fundamentals that I was practicing fifteen years ago. But the process and regimen of intense practice has increased the number of good shots I hit in a round and allowed me to manage my misses.

As an amateur golfer playing once or twice a week or less and practicing in intermittent spurts, the best you can hope for is to build a swing that has a chance of occasionally repeating, and managing a game that allows you to score well. You can also craft a game that minimizes the damage caused by your misses. But you will never eliminate missed shots and bad swings from your game—nobody ever has.

This might seem like depressing news, but it shouldn't be. Golf is a game you will never conquer, but neither will Tiger Woods, Annika Sorenstam, or any of the current crop of young stars emerging on the scene. With the right kind of practice, you can show substantial reductions in your scores and dramatic improvements in every aspect of your game.

Perfect Practice
Makes Perfect

The purpose of practicing your golf game is to groove good habits and build your game on sound fundamentals. But until you understand the fundamentals of the game, hours of practice won't do you much good. Practicing bad habits, poor technique, and faulty fundamentals is worse than not practicing at all, because you condition your muscles to perform the wrong motion. Once you've grooved these bad habits, reconditioning your muscles and your mind is harder and more time-consuming than if you had learned the correct technique from the beginning.

A great case in point is my most frustrating student, former NBA star Charles Barkley. Charles took up golf late in life, and because he is a great athlete, he played a lot of rounds and hit a lot of practice balls before he sought the advice of a professional instructor. By the time he came to me it was almost too late. Charles has two terrible hitches in his backswing, moves that are painful to watch but ones Charles has grooved through hours of practice. Were he not an athlete with exceptional eye-hand coordination, Charles would never get the golf ball airborne. What is even more frustrating to Charles and to those of us trying to teach him is that I could have saved him a lot of grief and sorrow if he had only come to me in the beginning. Now, with the bad habits so engrained in his muscle memory, it's a difficult uphill battle to get him making anything remotely resembling a golf swing.

You should learn a lesson from Sir Charles. Before you resolve to practice more, make sure you know what you should be practicing.

Start at the Hole
and Work Your Way Out

I believe all practice should begin on the putting green about one foot from the hole. Using your putter, you should get a feel for making contact with the ball, rolling it on the ground, and getting it into the hole from a short distance.

A lot of my students pooh-pooh this idea as too simple. A child can make a one-footer, they say, so why waste time working on such a simple little shot when it's the driver they need to swing.

"Ever heard of Phil Mickelson?" I ask them. Of course they have. Mickelson is a future Hall of Famer who many think is the greatest player in the world whose name isn't Tiger Woods. "Well," I continue, "Phil begins every practice session one foot from the hole. He's one of the best putters in the history of the game, but he still starts his practice at the hole, and he works his way outward."

You should make at least fifty to 100 putts from one foot before moving two or three feet away from the hole. In addition to the positive psychological effects of seeing the ball go in the hole, making a one-footer gives you a sense of feel, rhythm, grip pressure, and motion.

I know it sounds boring. You're probably saying to yourself, "Gosh, I make longer putts than that when I hit it through the dragon's mouth at Putt-Putt." But the one-foot drill is important for several reasons:

- *Distance Control.* You'd be stunned how many golfers hit a one-foot putt hard enough to send the ball traveling fifteen feet past the hole. Starting close to the hole gives you a feel for distance and allows you to make a small stroke, building a solid base on which to expand.

■ *A feel for grip and stance.*
Unless they grew up playing field hockey or softball, most women don't have any experience with what I call "ball and stick" games. That being the case, it's important that women begin their practice sessions reacquainting themselves with the feel for holding a club in their hands, positioning their bodies to hit a stationary ball lying on the ground in front of them.

It's also important to get accustomed to standing at a ninety-degree angle to the hole. In fact, that might be the toughest adjustment of all because it's so unnatural. If you're shooting pool, you face the table and (hopefully) the pocket where you want the ball to go. But in golf, you're facing Neverland—a place that is ninety degrees removed from where you want the ball to go. This is unnatural at its best and it can feel downright awkward. That's why so many women struggle with alignment. Practicing a short putt where the hole is visible in your peripheral vision sends alignment signals to your brain that will carry forward to longer putts and even to the full swing.

▲
Short putts like this give you a feel for distance control as well as a solid stroke.

■ *Building rhythm*. Golf is like a beautiful ballet, with each move choreographed to blend art and athleticism. That's why so many golfers study the swings of the game's greatest players. It's like watching and learning from a master dancer.

Of course the movements and positions of the body in dance mean nothing without the correct rhythm. The same is true for golf. Starting your practice sessions with the smallest shots in the game builds a sense of rhythm and timing that will carry forward throughout the rest of your game.

Moving Out

After making your one-footers, you should move out to three feet, then five feet, then ten, fifteen, and twenty feet, each time working on the rhythm of the stroke. Of course, if you make 100 twenty-footers give me a call. We need to get you on television.

The object of moving out is not to make every putt or even a majority of the putts from the longer distances. The drill is designed to give you the feel for slowly, methodically lengthening your stroke in order to hit the ball a little farther. Distance control becomes much tougher as the length of the putts increase. That's the point. By working outward from one foot to longer distances, you build on a solid foundation of feel.

Moving Off
the Green

When you gain a comfort level with the putter (and only you will know when you've reached that point), you should move ten to fifteen feet off the green and hit short bump shots with various clubs. These shots are extensions of your putts. You don't take the club back very far, nor do you make a full follow-through.

All you want to do is bunt the ball, getting the feel for the club swinging through the point of impact, that split second when club meets ball. The club swings like the pendulum of a grandfather clock through these shots, and the ball flies a short distance, then rolls toward the hole.

These shots prepare you for the full swing by giving you the feel for the hands, arms, shoulders, and body moving the club through the point of impact. If your hands are too active or your posture is poor or your arms, shoulders, and body aren't moving the club correctly, you'll know it. The ball will either roll on the ground, never getting in the air at all, or you will stick the club in the ground and move the ball only a few inches.

Believe it or not, these are good things. It's better to correct the mistakes that cause these kinds of mishaps while hitting short shots near the green. Once you progress to the full swing, it's a lot tougher to fix those same problems.

▲

Putting is unnatural, because you are not facing the hole.

◄

Move farther away from the hole as you gain confidence in your stroke.

Drills Are the Key

No one has ever sat down at the piano without a moment's practice and played a flawless concerto. No one has ever bowled a perfect game on her first try. And no golfer has ever grabbed a club out of the bag after a month layoff and played a perfect round of golf. It just doesn't happen, no matter how skilled and experienced you are. Without practice, your golf game gets rusty.

Practice doesn't always mean endlessly beating balls on the range. There are plenty of things you can do to train your body to make a good golf swing. Lee Brandon, the Women's World Long Drive champion who regularly hits drives over 300 yards, spends a great deal of time swinging a club in a swimming pool. "I came to golf from a fitness background, and I've always known that resistance training increases strength and speed," she says. "Water training works for sprinters and bodybuilders, why not golfers?"

She's right. Just because you can't commit to hitting 500 practice balls a day doesn't mean you can't drill your way to success in this game. Many of the world's greatest players have practice facilities at home, and many great amateur players keep practice tools in their homes and offices so they can keep their games sharp when they can't make it to the course. PGA Tour player Steve Elkington starts every day by rolling 100 putts in either his home in Houston or in his hotel room when he's on the road. It doesn't matter if Elk has a tee time later in the day or will be going to the course right after breakfast, he still practices at home to stay sharp and keep his putting stroke honed. Karrie Webb has a net in the garage of her Florida home even though the house is less

▶

Your first shots with a club other than the putter should be from a few feet off the green.

Beginners Should Take at Least Three Lessons Before Taking Their First Full Swing

If you take up golf on Friday and expect to run to the first tee on Saturday for an afternoon round with the girls, you're in for a shock. Learning golf is a long-term proposition. The reason most women exit the game after a short period isn't time constraints or frustration; it's embarrassment. They buy their clubs on Monday, take their first lesson on Tuesday, and sign up for the couples' tournament on Sunday where they promptly whiff the first three or four shots they attempt.

It doesn't have to be that way. If you're patient and disciplined enough to stay off the course for a while, you can learn the game properly and still have fun. I believe that every beginning woman golfer should take at least three lessons on and around the putting green—hitting short putts, long putts, chips, pitches, and short bump-and-run shots—before she ever takes a full swing.

When you interview and hire your teaching pro, you should insist on starting at the hole (or a foot or so away) and working your way back, taking at least three lessons over a two- to three-week period (with practice sessions in between) before you ever take a full swing. You should also map out a timeline with your professional that includes how much you intend to practice and what you will work on between lessons.

Does that mean you can't play golf for a month after starting? Technically, yes, but that doesn't mean you can't go out on the course and enjoy yourself. If you're a beginner and you get invited to play with a group, just say, "Hey, I'm a complete novice, but I'd love to walk around with you and putt and chip on a few holes." The group you're playing with won't care (in fact, they'll be delighted that you don't feel compelled to hit every shot on every hole), and you don't have to worry about the anxiety of whiffing it on the first tee.

than two minutes from a golf course. Karrie knows the importance of in-home practice, and she keeps the tools handy to keep her game sharp.

If practicing at home is good enough for the best players in the world, it's good enough for you. Some of the best practice drills for the home or office are:

■   *Putting for show.* If you don't have carpet in your home or office, an artificial strip of green with a hole carved into one end will cost you about $15. You won't learn how to read breaks, lag long putts, or gauge the speed of a slippery downhiller, but you will get comfortable setting up and stroking putts. Indoor putting helps you develop a good setup, good rhythm, and a stroke that rolls the ball end over end rather than scooting it along the ground. Plus you can do it while you're listening to the news or your favorite CD.

■   *Gripping a club for no apparent reason.* PGA Tour Commissioner Tim Finchem keeps a club near his desk in the tour's Ponte Vedra office, and every time he has a spare minute he picks up the club and checks his grip. To some this might look like a fidget, the commissioner's answer to doodling, but in reality it's a great indoor practice drill for developing and maintaining a consistent grip.

You should keep a club nearby in both your office and your home, and you should make a habit of gripping the club at least ten times a day. If you aren't comfortable with your grip, and you don't want to groove a bad habit, consider buying a preformed grip. These come in many shapes and sizes with grooves in the grip for your fingers. Preformed grips are illegal to play with, and

▼

Preformed grips aren't allowed on the course, but are great tools for learning the proper way to hold the club.

some of them don't work for people who have bigger- or smaller-than-average hands, but if you're looking for a tool to check your grip mechanics that you can keep around the house, these grips are worth looking into. They aren't just for beginners, either. LPGA player Jenny Lidback uses one regularly to check certain key points in her grip.

You should put a preformed grip on an old club and keep it in the corner of the kitchen or behind your desk at work. You'll be surprised how soon your grip will become second nature.

▼

Check your setup regularly by using a full-length mirror.

■ *Set up in front of a mirror.* Keep a club near your full-length mirror, whether that's in your bedroom, bathroom, kitchen, or office, and make a habit of going through your set-up routine in front of the mirror five to ten times a day. Seeing yourself set up will do wonders for your posture and ball position. Checking your posture from straight-on and side views will help you see and feel what a good golf setup should be.

■ *With your back against the wall.* Find a long empty wall somewhere in your home or office and set up so that your bottom touches the wall. Now swing a club slowly so that the clubhead never touches the wall. You should be able to go through your entire swing (slow motion, please, I don't want anyone knocking holes through their walls) without hitting the wall with the club. If you work on this drill fifteen or twenty times, you will begin to ingrain the sensation of swinging the club on plane (a concept I explain in more detail in a later chapter).

■ *Hitting balls into a net.* The Cadillac, Ferrari, Lexus, and every other luxury-car metaphor you can name of indoor practice is hitting balls into a net. This requires some space, like a garage, a basement, or a backyard, and an investment in hardware (a net and mat), but it is the ultimate indoor practice tool. Not only will your net allow you to hit real balls indoors, or in your yard, your swing will improve faster because you won't be overly concerned about the flight of the ball. You will focus on mechanics, not results. You'll see technical swing improvements quicker by practicing indoors than you would if you spent the same amount of time at the range.

Not everyone has the room or the wherewithal to install an indoor net, but for those who do, the results are dramatic. There's no better practice investment.

There are also plenty of drills you can take with you to the driving range. I remember the first time I saw Aree and Naree Wonglukiet, the sensational golfing twin girls from Thailand. They were practicing at the David Leadbetter Academy in Bradenton, Florida. Aree was wearing a Velcro harness that strapped her upper arms tightly to her torso and taking three-quarter swings, while Naree was hitting plastic balls that had been lined with a black Magic Marker. This didn't look like your typical practice session, but it was a standard part of the twins' routine. They worked on drills every day.

I use a number of teaching aids with my students as well, but I'll leave the gadget recommendations to your personal instructor. What I

The half-swing punch shot is a drill players of all skill levels should practice.

do want you to know is that drilling on the range is just as important as taking full swings and hitting an hour's worth of balls. A few drills you should incorporate into your regular practice sessions include:

■ *The half-swing drill*. Even the world's greatest players struggle with their swings on occasion, and when they do, one of the drills they fall back on is the half-swing punch shot, where your hands never get above hip-high in either direction. Setting up as you would for a regular shot then taking a half swing allows you to feel the big muscles of your back, shoulders, hips, and thighs, as well as your core muscles in your abdominal region rotate and react to the swing. It also gives you an opportunity to focus on making solid contact without worrying about distance, direction, or trajectory. By stripping off the trimming and focusing on the core move through impact, you gain confidence and feel for hitting the ball in the center of the clubface.

■ *Align clubs on the ground for practice*. Rarely does a practice session go by that I don't align two clubs parallel to each other on the ground, both pointing down the target line. This gives me a visual ref-

◀

Visual alignment tools are important for all players. A couple of clubs on the ground can make a world of difference.

erence for aligning my feet and the clubface, as well as a cue for the path of the swing through impact.

This is another drill you never grow out of. Vijay does it every time he practices; so does Dottie Pepper. It's an alignment cue, but it's also a guide to keep you from falling into bad habits like opening or closing your feet to the target, or swinging on a path other than the one leading down the target line. You would be well served by learning from the best in the game. Make a habit of putting clubs on the ground for alignment every time you practice.

▪   *Play an imaginary round on the range.* Because practice can be tedious business, I like to play games with myself to keep the process interesting. One of the best games I've found for the range is to play an imaginary round on the practice tee, starting with your driver and imagining you're on the first tee, then hitting the appropriate approach shot based on how well or how poorly you hit your tee shot. Two perfect shots in a row are counted as a birdie, but a poor drive or poor approach shot means bogey every time. Two poor shots in a row count as a double bogey. Keep score and keep records. You'll love to chart your improvement.

▪   *Up-and-down drill.* Another game is the up-and-down practice drill. Take ten balls to the chipping green and drop them in various spots around the perimeter. Then pick a hole and try to get every ball up and down in no more than two strokes, one chip and one putt. Hole them all and keep score. If you shoot a 20 you're an expert; 22 to 25 and you're pretty good; and a 30 or higher means you need to work on your short game.

These are just a few of the hundreds of practice drills out there. Your professional will have his or her own suggestions based on your specific needs. The important thing is to incorporate drills into your regular practice sessions. They work. You will improve if you spend time drilling for success.

Practice Pitfalls

S ome people don't get better no matter how much they practice. That's not a law of nature; it's just a fact. These people either practice bad swing habits—flaws they carry with them onto the golf course—or they practice in ways that don't benefit their games. Some of the more basic concepts to consider when setting up a practice schedule include:

■ *Try not to hurt yourself.* I know people (men, mostly, but some women) who don't practice or play for weeks, then show up on the range armed with hundreds of balls as if cramming a month's worth of practice into one session will make up for all the days they skipped. This never works. For starters, golf is, contrary to what some might say, an athletic endeavor. And like all athletic endeavors, fatigue sets in after a while and you get sloppy. Tired tennis players don't hit crisp groundstrokes and their serves aren't as fast and as sharp as they were earlier in the match, and tired golfers make sloppy swings and groove bad habits.

Injury is also a concern. If your muscles aren't conditioned to hitting hundreds of balls a day, going out with a laundry basket full of range balls is like running in a marathon after jogging around the block a few times for training. You're going to hurt yourself. The most common repetitive-motion injuries involve the rotator cuff and the lower back, but your hands, arms, legs, and sides can also be affected.

It's much better to practice one hour a day, three days a week than to practice one day a week for three hours. Once you get yourself into "golf shape" you can incrementally extend your practice sessions as long as you don't cut down on the frequency. Steady, incremental practice will not only improve your game faster; it's better for your health.

- *Practice when you're hitting it well.* Too many players hit a few good shots on the range and say to themselves or out loud to those around them, "I don't need to waste those out here. I need to take shots like that to the golf course," and off they go. Or an even better line comes when a player hits one good practice shot. "I can't hit it any better than that, so I'd better quit," she says.

This logic is asinine. The purpose of practicing is to groove good golf swings, to condition your muscles and your mind to the correct swing motion and repeat that motion enough times that it becomes second nature, like holding a fork, typing, or playing a musical instrument. You practice golf so your body gets used to making good swings. When you're on the golf course you don't have to think about swing mechanics. Your body remembers what to do from all the practice you've put in, and you repeat the preconditioned motion of the swing.

When you hit a few good shots, you shouldn't stop practicing. That's the time you should practice more! You want to groove good swings. When you're swinging well, your timing is right, and your confidence is high. You shouldn't walk away from the range; you should spend some extra time conditioning your body to remember that feeling.

If you only travel to the range when you're hitting the ball poorly, and you stop practicing the minute you hit a few good shots, you aren't improving. Good players practice when they're hitting it good. That's part of what makes them good players.

■ *Warm up before you play; practice afterward.* I'm all for spending an hour or two on the range, but putting in that kind of practice time before you go out on the course isn't the best thing for your scores. In addition to being tired before you get to the first tee, this sort of intense practice tends to leave your mind cluttered with swing thoughts—baggage you don't need to carry onto the course.

Preround practice should be limited to no more than fifty range balls with the primary emphasis on warming up and loosening your muscles. This is the time for working on rhythm and getting one or two key swing thoughts to take with you onto the course. It's not the time to over-

▼

Play up-and-down games with yourself to improve your short game.

haul your swing or beat hundreds of balls to groove something new. If you don't have it an hour before teeing off, chances are you won't find it in the last minutes.

After your round is a much better time to venture onto the range. You're loose and warm from your round, and you should have a good idea what areas of your game require the most attention. This is the practice strategy all tour players employ, and it's one that will work wonders for you as well.

■ *One lesson won't cut it.* Too often students take one lesson and head to the first tee convinced they now understand all the mystic secrets of golf. This is unadulterated wackiness. If Tiger Woods couldn't learn everything he needed to know about golf in a year or two years or even ten years, why would someone who plays twice a month think she can master golf's idiosyncrasies in one lesson?

Lessons are an important component to your practice regimen. Just as the pianist needs to go back for a lesson or a little coaching every so often regardless of the amount of practice she puts in, so too does the golfer need a regularly scheduled checkup. Building monthly or quarterly lessons into your practice program will insure that you stay on course and continue steadily improving.

Practice Tips

Without watching your swing and evaluating your abilities, I can't tell you exactly what you should practice and how long you should stay on the range. But I can give you some universal practice tips that will help you get the most out of your practice sessions. They are:

- *Go to the end of the range.* Golf is an insular game. No matter what else is going on around you, the moment of truth boils down to you, the club, and the ball. Nobody else matters. That's why the most effective practice sessions are when you're alone on the range. Unfortunately, you can't always control when and where other people want to practice. More often than not you're going to have to share the range with your fellow golfers.

   You can still isolate yourself by moving to the end of the range so that you have your back to the other players. This helps you focus more on your game without the distractions of seeing other people. You might appear antisocial, but that's the point. You're there to practice golf, not chitchat. Moving to the end of the range and working on your swing sends a clear signal to others that you are serious about your practice time.

- *Practice with specific goals.* Beating balls for its own sake is a waste of time. You should enter every practice session with a goal. If your instructor has given you one fundamental or one key swing to work on, spend the day working on that one thing. Don't jump from one goal to the next in the middle of a practice session. You'll lose your

▶

Regular visits
with your instructor
will shorten your
learning curve.

focus and waste your time. Always go the range saying, "Today I'm going to work on X." And spend your time doing just that.

■ *Take regular breaks and evaluate your progress.* Even the most ardent practice fanatics regularly step back and evaluate their progress. No one practices longer and harder than Vijay, but he doesn't hit balls endlessly without stopping and checking his progress. All good players take regular practice breaks where they evaluate where they are, where they want to be, and the progress they're making toward their ultimate goals.

■ *Devote at least sixty percent of your practice time to the short game.* The difference between a good player who practices two hours a day and a mediocre to poor player who puts in the same amount of practice is that the good player spends over an hour of that practice time hitting short shots, chips, pitches, and putts. The mediocre or poor player will spend an hour flailing away with a driver, and if she hits one or two putts it's as an oh-by-the-way afterthought.

Between sixty and sixty-five percent of all shots in a round are played from 100 yards and in. You should devote a proportionate amount of time to practicing those shots.

Practicing shouldn't be like drudgery. You should gain joy by seeing improvement in your game, and you should feel good about the work you're putting into such a productive endeavor. Perfect practice produces its own rewards. The self-confidence you gain from steady improvement in your swing and consistent lowering of your scores will transcend golf and make you feel better about yourself as you go through your everyday life.

PART TWO:

Fundamentals
of the Game

IN ANY ROUND OF GOLF, no matter how well you play, about half the shots you hit will be putts. That makes putting the most important part of the game by a mile. Tour players keep their putts-per-round statistics in the twenty-seven to twenty-eight putt range for every eighteen holes they play. That averages out to be around forty percent of the total

4 Putting: The Game Within the Game

shots per round, which is great, but it's still a higher percentage than any other aspect of the game.

Since putting represents half the shots you're likely to play in any given round, it stands to reason that if your putting improves, you will score better, even if the rest of your game remains unchanged. I think the late, great teacher Harvey Penick put it best when he said, "A good putter is a match for any man. A bad putter is a match for no one." That is simple, unassailable logic. Everybody should understand the value of being a good putter. But, to my constant amazement, a lot of people don't get it—especially women.

I think Penick's simple axiom is especially appropriate where women are concerned. I believe women don't putt as well as they could or should. This applies to everyone from touring professionals to the high-handicap amateurs who play weekly matches at clubs all over the country. Women as a group don't putt as well as men, which is a shame since strength has no bearing on how well you putt.

Putting is about feel and rhythm, two aspects of the game where women should excel. Unfortunately we don't, and I believe it's because of misplaced priorities. Women want to hit the ball farther. We want to impress our playing partners with our prodigious length, and we want to hear things like, "Wow, she hits it so far! I wonder how she does it?" So we spend hours on the practice tee working on our swings, doing everything we can to eke out a few extra yards. Putting becomes an afterthought.

Nothing could be more wrongheaded. Sure, if you work for years on your long game, hitting hundreds of balls a day and working out in the gym to improve your strength and flexibility, you might stretch your drives farther than most amateur men. But there isn't a woman alive who will reach Tiger Woods-type length. Laura Davies is the longest hitter in the women's game, and even she will tell you that she'll never hit it as far as Tiger or David Duval or Vijay Singh or her good friend John Daly. Laura will also tell you that it doesn't matter how far she hits it if she doesn't putt well. Getting the ball in the hole is what the game is all about, and putting is where that happens. Relegating putting to oh-by-the-way status is illogical, and it hurts our ability to score.

The best and most tragic example of what I've just described was the fate of former U.S. Women's Amateur champion Vicki Goetz-Ackerman. Vicki grew up playing golf in Athens, Georgia, where she spent hours on the putting green. By age ten, she would insist on making ten ten-footers in a row before going home. Her dad would sometimes pull the car up to the green and shine the headlights on the hole so Vicki could see to practice.

The hard work paid off. Vicki won two U.S. Women's Amateurs, was the low amateur in three U.S. Women's Opens, won the 1992 NCAA championship, and made the cut in nine out of twelve LPGA events she played in as an amateur. She quickly became known as one of the best putters in the women's game, even before she turned pro.

But there were rumblings. Word filtered through the tour that Vicki couldn't compete at the professional level because she wasn't long enough. Forget that she competed in the toughest tournament in women's golf, the U.S. Women's Open, by hitting fairways and making putts; the rap on Vicki was that she didn't have enough length.

If Vicki had ignored those comments and stuck with her "hit it short and make every putt" approach, she might have been more successful. But she let the criticism get to her, and she spent her first seven years on tour trying to increase her distance. Her putting suffered as a result, and Vicki never reached the potential she had shown as an amateur.

Half the Shots Require Half the Time

Since putting constitutes half the number of shots you're likely to play in a round, it stands to reason that you should spend half your practice time with a putter in your hands. I believe that every golfer—beginners, intermediates, and professionals—should start each practice and warm-up session on the putting green.

Starting with your putter gets you in a rhythm and keeps you cognizant of the ball going into the hole. It also keeps that part of your game in the forefront. When you begin your practice sessions on the driving range you run the risk of getting caught up in working with one or two clubs. Before you know it, you're out of time and you haven't rolled a single putt. If you start all practice on the putting green, you've eliminated that potential problem.

Gripping the Putter

There is no firm and fast rule of how to put your hands on the putter, as evidenced by some of the wacky grips used by pros and amateurs alike. Mark Calcavecchia and Chris DiMarco turn their right hands over on top of the shaft like you would if you were grabbing a hammer. They call their grip "the claw," and while I wouldn't recommend it to the majority of my students, it certainly works for Chris and Mark.

Beth Daniel has experimented with almost every conceivable grip as well. She went cross-handed (or "left-hand low") for a while. Then she tried pressing the shaft of the putter against her left forearm and holding it there with her right hand. When that didn't work, Beth switched to an extra-long putter, one she holds under her chin with her left hand while moving the club back and forth through the stroke with her right hand. This is a classic example of the "whatever works" theory of putting. If holding the end of the putter in your mouth would guarantee a solid stroke and more made four-footers, thousands of golfers would be opening wide and checking their dental work.

The two most common putter grips, and the ones I recommend to my students are:

- *Reverse overlap grip.* This is the most commonly used putting grip, because it's so similar to the grip most golfers use on the rest of their clubs. With your palms facing each other, your right hand lower than your left, place the grip of the putter diagonally across your hands from the pad of your hands to the first knuckle of your index fingers. Then place both thumbs on top of the grip and close your hands lightly. All ten fingers should be on the club at this stage, and the thumb of your left hand should be resting comfortably between the crevice formed by the pad and palm of your right hand.

Now to complicate things a little, take the index finger of your left hand and move it on top of the pinkie finger and ring finger of your right hand. This will bring your hands closer together, which is the point.

The purpose of any golf grip is to make the hands work as a single unit. You don't want your left hand or right hand dominating the putting stroke (or the full swing for that matter). In golf the hands work as one, and the grip is the way you insure that unity.

The other reason for this seemingly convoluted hand position is, believe it or not, tension. This overlapping grip allows you to control the club with a minimum amount of grip pressure. If you're gripping the club properly, you don't have to strangle it in order to control it. You can relax your grip pressure without fear of the club slipping or turning in your hands. This light grip pressure is crucial, because putting is about feel. If you've put a death grip on your putter, you can't feel anything, and the likelihood of making a two-foot putt becomes slim. With light hands, your touch improves. Your grip facilitates that.

- *Left-hand-low.* An increasingly popular putting grip is the "left-hand-low" or "cross-handed" grip, where the position of the hands is reversed. The palms still face each other, but the left hand is lower than the right, and the pinkie of the left hand overlaps the index finger of the right.

Annika Sorenstam uses this grip sometimes, and Fred Couples has been putting this way for years. Before going to a longer putter, Vijay Singh won the Masters putting left-hand-low, and Jan Stephenson and Kelly Robbins swear that the grip saved their games.

▲
Reverse overlap and left-hand-low are two of the most popular (and productive) putting grips.

Glove-Free Putting

- -

One of my students, who is the wife of a prominent and somewhat famous business executive, refuses to take off her glove while she's putting. "That's a giveaway that you're not a very accomplished player," I said to her. "Putting is about feel. In order to maximize your feel, you want to have both hands on the putter."

"I can't do it," she said.

"Sure you can," I replied. "Just take the glove off when your ball is on the green, fold it in half with the fingers facing the palm, and put it in your back pocket or in the waistline of your shorts. It's easy."

"No, no," she said. "I know how to take my glove off. I just can't putt without a glove. It feels funny."

I didn't say anything else, but I knew the subject would come up again. A few weeks later during the Baltimore Senior Classic I found myself paired with my student and Christie O'Connor, Jr., the great Irish professional. Two holes into our round, Christie pulled me aside and said, "So, what's with the glove while she's putting?"

"I've tried, Christie," I said.

A few holes later Christie couldn't hold his tongue any longer. "You know," he said to my student, "you would putt a lot better if you took off your glove. These greens are fast, and fast greens require great feel. You're handicapping yourself by wearing a glove on the green. You might as well try putting in boxing gloves."

My student cut her eyes toward me to see if Christie and I had conspired against her. I shrugged and shook my head. The truth was the truth, no matter who the messenger was.

Despite those proclamations, there's no magic to the left-hand-low grip. It simply helps some players use their hands as a single unit, the same goals and objectives of the reverse overlap, the claw, the split-hand (where the hands are several inches apart on the club) or any other grip.

After years of bad putting, one of my students finally agreed to give left-hand-low a try. "It feels awful," she said.

- -

"Just give it a few days, and see if the ball rolls off the putter any truer for you," I said. Sure enough, a week later she was back singing the grip's praises.

"It's great," she said. "There's no bounce or scoot now. The ball rolls right off the putter blade."

For this student, the left-hand-low grip was the answer. It may or may not be the answer for you. If it works, fine. If it doesn't, try something else. Putting is one of the most personal parts of the game because to do it well requires you to be comfortable. If a left-hand-low grip makes you feel better, by all means give it a try.

Poor Posture Produces Pitiful Putting

I try to emphasize positives and cut down on negatives when I'm teaching, but the alliteration of all of those Ps was just too tempting to pass up. A positive way of saying the same thing is, "Good posture is critical to good putting," but somehow that's not quite as catchy.

You get the point. If your posture is good, you have a good chance of making a good stroke. If your posture is bad, your stroke, your touch, your talent, and your timing mean nothing. You aren't going to putt well with poor posture.

I believe that the good posture and good setup in golf aren't much different from the athletic posture you would assume to shoot a free throw in basketball or to catch a ground ball in softball or to play defense in soccer. To do any of those things, you need to position your feet shoulder-width apart. Your weight should be evenly distributed on

▲

Poor putting posture:
too upright, too
slouched, too far away
from the ball.

the balls of your feet, your knees flexed, your back straight, and your torso bent slightly forward. This is a good athletic position, the same position a coach would recommend for almost any sport.

A lot of women have posture problems. The most common faults I see are women standing erect and rigid, almost as if they are at attention, or women slumping their shoulders and rounding their backs. After years of study I've discovered why women (more so than men) tend to lapse into these poor setup positions. Setting up properly, with your knees bent, your back straight, and your torso tilted forward, gives you the sensation that you are sticking your rear end out, a very unladylike thing to do out of doors. When I put many of my female students in the correct setup position, they feel self-conscious, as if everyone is staring at them because of the provocative way in which they are standing.

The fact is, good putting posture feels a lot funnier than it looks. To prove it, try setting up with a full-length mirror nearby. You'll find

that what feels like an unattractive protrusion of your lower quarters is
really beautiful posture for putting.

Ball Position

believe in positioning the ball in a spot somewhere between the middle of your stance (directly between your feet) and just inside your
left foot. From this position you can place the putter head behind
the ball, keeping the shaft of the club fairly straight, without having to
manipulate your hands. If the ball were any farther forward, your
hands would be behind the ball and an unnatural angle would form
between your left arm and the shaft of the putter. Any farther back
and the hands would be too far ahead of the ball.

    Ball position is important because you want to be able to roll the
ball toward the hole with as little manipulation of the putter as possi-

▼

Ball off the right foot
(too far from back),
off left toe (too far
forward), inside your
left heel (just right).

▲

Eyes outside the ball;
eyes inside the ball;
eyes directly over the
ball—just right.

ble. If the ball is too far back in your stance, your natural tendency is to hit down on it, causing the ball to pop up in the air and skid off-line. If the ball is too far forward in your stance, you have unwittingly added loft to the putter, which could cause the ball to jump off-line at impact.

A slightly forward-of-center ball position is perfect, because it allows you to move the putter back and through the shot with minimum muss and fuss.

Eyes Over the Ball

Women seem to have great difficulty deciding how far away from the ball they need to stand. I've seen some women stand so close to the ball I'm amazed they can make contact without hitting themselves. I've also seen women stand so far away they need a broom just to reach the ball.

I can't tell you how far away from the ball you need to stand in inches or feet, but a good rule of thumb is to play the ball just below your eyes. A good way to test your ball position is to set up to stroke a putt, then take an extra ball out of your pocket, place it against your left eyelid, and drop it to the ground. If the ball you drop doesn't hit the ball on the ground you're about to putt, you need to adjust your stance accordingly.

CINDY'S INTERMEDIATE TIP

Move Farther Away When Putting Goes Awry

One of the best putting tips I ever heard came from Davis Love III. According to Davis's theory, every player, regardless of skill, will experience putting slumps, times when your touch leaves you, you can't see the line, and your stroke feels awkward. Sometimes these slumps can occur in the middle of a round. You're putting good, feeling great, when suddenly you find yourself struggling over a two-footer.

"When that happens, I back away from the ball a little more," Davis says. "This frees up my arms, so I can make a more fluid stroke. It also improves my posture so I can see the line a lot better."

When I find myself struggling with my putting during a round, I find Davis's theory works great. By moving a little farther away from the ball at address, I'm able to find the line that seemed so elusive only moments before. Now, whenever I'm struggling with my putting in the middle of a round, I back away a few inches. The results are not always magical, but it helps more often than it hurts.

The Stroke

The putting stroke is, as the name implies, a stroke. It is not a punch, push, jab, hit, swat, or slap. It's a smooth, orderly, compact, straight-back-and-straight-through stroke. Since the first day I took up the game I've heard instructors compare the putting stroke to the pendulum of a grandfather clock, a one-piece motion that goes back and through. That analogy is well worn because it's good.

▲

The arms and putter work like the pendulum of a grandfather clock.

Good putters have smooth pendulum-like putting strokes that seem as fluid and effortless as the hypnotic swaying of the arm inside your grandmother's parlor clock.

You've seen players with such strokes. Karrie Webb, Lori Kane, Ben Crenshaw, Tiger Woods, Juli Inkster, and Justin Leonard all have such simple, fluid putting strokes it looks as if they were born to be good putters. But these flawless fluid strokes don't come naturally. They are the result of endless hours of hard work.

For starters, all golfers have to overcome the natural tendency to "hit" the golf ball. This is true in the full swing as well, but it's especially pertinent in putting. Your instincts are almost overpowering. The club is in your hands; you hit the ball with the club; therefore you have to use your hands to move the club to hit the ball. Makes sense, right?

Unfortunately, nothing could be worse for your putting stroke. Go to any beginner clinic or even to any miniature golf course and you'll see what I mean. People who aren't interested in learning proper technique will invariably slap at balls with their hands, and you'll see balls rolling all over the place. If one happens to find the hole, it's purely by accident. Not only can you not control where your putts are going with that sort of stroke, you'll never be able to gauge distance and speed. Sure, you might make a putt or two—a spendaholic stumbles onto a bargain every now and then—but you'll never be a consistently good putter until you take your hands out of the stroke.

The best putters initiate their strokes by turning their shoulders back and forth like a teeter-totter. This keeps the putter and your arms moving as one piece. Jack Nicklaus always said it was like the putter and your arms formed a Y and your job was to make sure that Y remained intact throughout the stroke. It's hard to argue with Jack.

Women like Dottie Pepper and Se Ri Pak, both outstanding putters, subscribe to that same philosophy, and it's evident in their strokes. Like all good putters, these women keep their heads and their lower bodies perfectly still. The only movement is in their shoulders and arms. Some, like Annika Sorenstam, don't even move their eyes until the ball is fully three feet off the putter head and rolling toward the hole.

There are a lot of talented golfers who spend their entire golfing lives trying to keep their heads and bodies still and take their hands out of the stroke. Beth Daniel thinks she developed the "yips" (the inability to make anything from ten feet in) because of jumpy eyes. She let her vision lead the stroke, and it created all sorts of problems. My friend Vijay Singh became so frustrated by his inability to keep his Y from breaking down that he now uses an extra-long putter that he sticks into his sternum for support. Even Vijay would tell you that his solution is a little radical, but it works. Hopefully you can keep your body still and make a smooth, connected stroke without resorting to such extremes.

Some drills to help you learn this stroke include:

- *The railroad track drill*. Place two clubs on the ground parallel to each other like the rails on a railroad track with just enough room between the clubs for the head of your putter. Then practice rolling putts between the tracks so that your putter doesn't hit either golf club, and the ball rolls straight out of the tracks.

- *The taping-of-the-wrist drill*. A lot of people can't feel their wrists breaking during a stroke. They swear that they're making a one-piece stroke and that their Ys are intact throughout, but an outside observer can see the hands taking over and the wrists breaking down. One way to give yourself the feel of a solid, one-piece stroke is to run a

▲
Railroad track drill keeps the putter moving down the line.

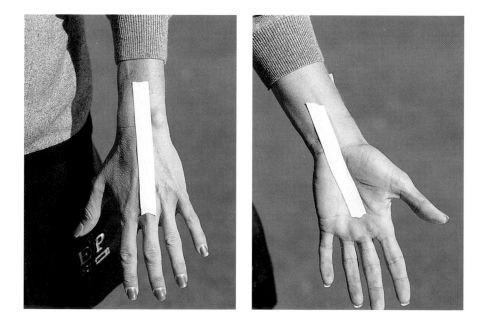

▶
Tape your left wrist to keep it from breaking down during the stroke.

strip of masking tape from your left palm up the inside of your left forearm. Apply the tape so that it's taut when there is no bend in your left wrist.

Now roll a few putts. If your hands are taking over and slapping at the ball during your putting stroke, you will feel the tape pull on your hand and arm. When you can roll putts without dislodging or pulling on the tape, you know you're making a solid stroke.

- *The left-hand-only drill.* While there are many causes for breakdowns in putting, one of the most common is when your right hand overpowers your left hand at the moment of impact. This slapping action doesn't have to be pronounced to cause major problems. Slight hits or jerks at the moment club meets ball can pull or push your putts off-line.

To condition your body against such actions, try rolling putts with only your left hand on the club. This forces you to concentrate on a solid, one-piece, back-and-through stroke.

◄ Left-hand-only putting smooths out a choppy stroke.

Following Through on Good Putting

I f you ever watch tapes of old golf matches, those played prior to about 1970, you'll notice a big difference in the way players putted then and the way they putt now. Back in the "old days" before advances in agronomy and irrigation, grass was longer and thicker than it is today. As a result, the speeds balls rolled on the greens were much slower. Players had to rap putts pretty hard at times just to get the ball to the hole. That was reflected in the short, popping strokes players used on the greens. Players like Patty Berg and Betsy Rawls were masters at this wristy, popping stroke, and during that period, it worked.

Today, greens are faster and better manicured, and the jab stroke has gone the way of the hickory shaft. Players who failed to make the transition—like Billy Casper, who was one of the greatest putters in the world—found themselves unable to judge speed.

Faster greens require more fluid strokes, strokes where the follow-through is just as important to the rhythm and timing of the putt as the setup and takeaway. Tom Watson, who was a fabulous putter in his prime, used to say that in order to putt well your follow-through needed to be at least twice as long as your takeaway. Later in his career Tom struggled with short putts because he abandoned his own theory and his stroke got short and quick.

If you look at all great putters today, you will find they all have great follow-throughs. The putter goes straight back and continues toward the hole after impact.

There are a couple of drills that can help you with your follow-through, which will improve the timing, rhythm, and consistency of your stroke.

■ *Look at the hole.* One of the best putting drills to teach the feel and rhythm of the stroke is to look at the hole rather than at the ball while you putt. From ten to fifteen feet away, set up as though you are going to make your normal stroke, but just before you are ready to stroke the putt, turn your head and your eyes so that you are looking at the hole. Then stroke the putt without looking back at the ball.

The results will seem like magic. Not only will your stroke become smoother and more consistent after you work on this drill for a while, you will instinctively increase your follow-through.

Some players actually use this for short putts while playing competitive rounds. I don't recommend that, but I do recommend that you spend several hours on the putting green looking at the hole instead of the ball.

When I recommended this drill to one of my good-player students, she said, "I can't do that. I'll miss the ball!"

"Just give it a try," I said. "You might be surprised."

Indeed she was surprised. Not only did she not mishit any of the putts, she made six fifteen-foot putts in a row while looking at the hole. I can't guarantee the same results for you, but it's certainly worth a try.

▼

Putt while looking at the hole to develop feel.

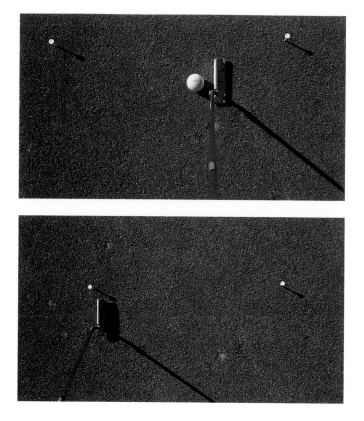

▲

Visual cues—like tees in the ground—will help you follow through with your putting stroke.

■ *Mark your stroke with tees.* Visual cues often serve as great mental reminders of what you need to do in your golf swing and in your putting stroke. When I find students getting a little short and quick with their putting strokes, I'll place two tees in the ground on a line just outside the intended line of the putt. I put one of the tees six to eight inches behind the ball, and the other a foot or more ahead of the ball. Then I tell my student to take the putter back only as far as the back tee, but follow through all the way to the forward tee.

This is a little awkward and distracting at first, but after a few minutes, you forget about the tees, even though they remain in your peripheral vision and continue to provide a mental cue to follow through with your stroke.

Line and Speed,
the Art of Reading Putts

Now that you know how to grip the putter, set up to a putt, and make a decent stroke, the ball should automatically go in the hole, right? Oh, if it were only that easy! The hardest part of putting isn't setting up and making the stroke; the hardest part is picking the correct line and speed on which to hit the putt.

Golf greens are not pool tables. They have slopes, humps, bumps, and lumps, some of which look like roller coasters when you're trying to putt them. A putt that gets on the wrong side of one of those humps can run farther away from the hole than you were when you started. That's why line and speed are the two most important aspects of putting, with speed edging out line as the most critical element to making good putts.

If you misread the line of a putt—that is, if you think the slope of the green will force a ball to curve a particular way when in fact the ball breaks the opposite direction—you will miss the putt by the amount of break you misread, assuming you hit the putt the right speed. So, if you think a putt breaks three inches left, but it breaks one inch right, you will miss the putt by four inches if you hit it the correct speed. If you hit it the wrong speed, however, you can miss it by as much as ten feet.

A ball hit the wrong speed has little chance of going in and a great chance of stopping several feet short of the hole or running several feet past the hole. A putt hit the right speed has a great chance of going in, even if the line isn't perfect (balls fall in the sides of holes all the time), and the worst that will happen is you will miss the putt by the amount of break you have misplayed.

As simple and logical as that sounds, most amateur golfers never consider the speed of their putts. They crouch down and look at the line, shielding their eyes from the sunlight and analyzing slopes (real and imagined) between their balls and the hole without a moment's thought of the speed. What most golfers, particularly women, don't realize is that the line of a putt varies depending on the speed. If you hit a putt harder, and the ball is rolling faster, gravity has less of an impact, and the putt breaks less. If you hit the putt softly and slowly, the ball will take the fall line of the green much quicker and the putt will break more. The line of any putt is actually a trough. You can hit

CINDY'S INTERMEDIATE TIP

The "Play It Right Here" Advice

One of the most commonly offered pieces of advice women hear on the golf course is the "Play it right here" tip on the green. You're standing over a putt, calculating the line and speed you need for your shot when someone (usually one of the overly helpful men in your group) marches up to the hole, points to a spot on the ground a few inches outside the hole, and says, "Play it right here."

I know they mean well, but the people who offer this advice drive me nuts. How can you tell people where to play a putt when you have no idea how hard they plan on hitting the shot. If I have an uphill putt on a slow green, I might want to strike the putt firmly, taking most of the break out of the putt, and slamming it into the back of the hole. If I have a slippery down-hiller, I might want to coax the putt slowly over the front edge of the hole. Either of these strategies is fine, but they dramatically affect how much the putt is going to break, which makes the "Play it right here" advice worthless.

No one can tell you which line to take on a putt without knowing how hard you plan to hit it. Sure, you can get some help if you're having trouble reading the break. But having someone point to a spot and say "Play it right here" is useless.

the ball anywhere within that trough and it has a chance of going in the hole if it has been struck with the proper speed.

I illustrate this all the time in my short-game clinics. Picking a side-hill six-footer, I hit a couple of putts firmly, playing only a couple of inches of break. If I'm lucky, one of the balls hits the back of the hole and drops in. But the putt only breaks two inches or so. Then I hit the same putt with a much slower pace, but playing a foot or more of break. These shots roll slowly up the edge of the hole. Some fall in, other's don't, but the break of these putts is significantly greater than the putts struck with more speed.

For some reason women have a terrible time comprehending the importance of speed, and an even more difficult time implementing that concept once they've figured it out. That one fact above all others is why women don't putt as well as they should.

It doesn't have to be that way. Here are a couple of drills that will help you with the speed of your putts.

- *Putt to a larger circle.* The hole is only four-and-a-quarter inches in diameter. From twenty or thirty feet it can look like a thimble. But a two-foot circle around the hole looks as big as a washtub by comparison. With either string or chalk, you should draw a two-foot circle around a particular hole on the putting green, and from twenty, thirty, and forty feet, you should work on rolling every putt inside that much larger two-foot circle. Don't worry about making the putt. If you focus on noth-

▼
Putting to a larger circle from long distances improves your feel and eliminates the dreaded three-putt.

ing more than getting every putt inside your circle, you'll be shocked how many of those long putts go in the hole, and you will be amazed how easy the tap-ins are that you've left yourself even if you miss.

■ *Lay a club eighteen inches behind the hole.* One of golf's oldest jokes—attributed to Lee Trevino, but probably around since golfers played in plaid knickers and ties—says that ninety-nine percent of the putts you leave short don't go in. Women have a terrible tendency to leave putts short, more so than men or junior golfers. To get women accustomed to getting all their putts to the hole, I have my students lay a golf club eighteen inches behind the hole and putt at the hole from fifteen to twenty feet away. I want my students to make the putt, but more important, those putts that don't go in should roll all the way to the golf club. That means that a missed putt should roll eighteen inches past the hole.

This drill teaches my female students how to roll the ball past the hole, an important concept in judging the speed of long putts on the golf course.

Once you have figured out how to judge speed, the next element is picking a line for the putt. This requires an ability to see topographical changes in the landscape and to intuitively or analytically determine how those changes will affect a ball rolling on a particular line at a particular speed.

It sounds more complicated than it is. If the landscape slopes severely from right to left between your ball and the hole, it stands to reason that your putt is going to break left. How much the putt will break given the speed you want to hit it is something only practice and experience can show you.

There is one drill I like to prescribe to my students for learning how to read the break.

- *Practice in a five-foot circle.* Pick a hole on the putting green that is either situated on or surrounded by a substantial slope and place between six and ten balls in a five-foot circle around the hole. Some of the balls will be on the slope above the hole and some will be below the hole, while still others will be positioned across the slope. By putting around the circle, trying to roll each of the five-foot putts in the hole, you experience every type of break, and you get a feel for reading breaking putts.

▲

This is golf's equivalent of a basketball shoot-around. Making putts from a five-foot circle around the hole builds confidence and improves your fundamentals.

Putting Games That Make Practice Fun

know that standing on the putting green and rolling three-footers for hours on end isn't exactly award-winning entertainment. It's not even particularly healthy. An hour-long cycle class at the gym might not be fun either, but at least you can feel good about having gotten a workout. Putting can be hot, boring work. But there are some games you can play with yourself to make practice more interesting.

- *Reverse ladder.* Pick one hole on the putting green and put tees in the ground at one-foot intervals behind that hole all the way out to ten feet. Starting next to the one-foot tee, roll a one-foot putt in the hole,

Good Players Should Practice Putting to a Tee

If you've ever attended an LPGA event and watched the greatest women golfers in the world practice, you've probably seen more than a few of them placing tees in the putting green and rolling putts to the tee. This isn't because the green is too crowded and no holes are available. Good players should practice putting to smaller targets, like a tee or a small coin. If you can putt your ball to something the size of a tee or a coin, the hole will look like a washtub.

A few pros who have practice greens in their yards cut smaller-than-standard holes in the ground for practice purposes. If they can learn to make putts into the smaller holes, the standard holes will look like canyons when they get out on the course.

Few amateurs have the luxury of putting greens in their backyards, but the principle still applies. Putting to a tee or a coin will hone your stroke, improve your focus, and make you a better putter when you get out on the course.

then move back to the two-foot tee and make the putt from there. Then move back to the three-foot tee and make that putt and so on until you make the ten-footer. The catch is, if you miss any putt from any distance, you have to start over at the one-foot mark.

There's no pressure in the world like standing over that ten-footer to end the game after having worked at this for over an hour. But it's also a fun game that will help you develop into a great putter.

■ *Nine-hole game.* Pick out nine holes on the putting green and design your own putting course. Then keep score for nine holes and see how you do. The catch is, if you three-putt any hole on your course, you have to add a penalty shot to your score for that hole. Anything more than eighteen putts for nine holes is unacceptable. If you start scoring 14 or better for eighteen holes, try lengthening your course.

Challenge yourself, but make it fun. You can even hold tournaments with yourself where ball A plays ball B in a grudge match to determine Putting Champion of the World.

How good a putter you become is directly related to how much effort you put into learning and practicing the craft. But you can't be a great player unless you become a good putter. There's no reason you can't do it. Strength and athleticism have no bearing. The only thing holding you back is you.

Remember: A good putter is a match for anyone.

BECAUSE GOLF IS A BALL-AND-STICK GAME, the only contact you the golfer have with the ball is through the club, and your only contact with the club is through your hands. That's why I call the grip—the placement of the hands on the golf club—the First Fundamental. It's your first and only line of contact with the golf club, and it's the foundation on which all other aspects of the swing are built. With a good grip a lot of the other movements and positions you want to achieve during the golf swing fall into place pretty quickly. With a bad grip, you're doomed from the start. No amount of practice will overcome the problems you'll face if you grip the club poorly.

5 Gripping the Club: The First Fundamental

This is especially true for women. Like it or not, our hands aren't as strong as those of most men. We don't have the luxury of overcoming mistakes in our grips through brute force. Women have to be diligent in the details of this First Fundamental, and we have to work hard to make holding a golf club correctly as natural as holding the phone or gripping the steering wheel of a car. When a good grip becomes second nature, you can focus on other aspects of your game with greater confidence.

Why Is the Grip
So Important?

A lot of my students wonder why every golf instructor they talk to starts every discussion with the grip. "It's just putting your hands on the club," the students say. "What's the big deal?"

The grip is crucial because it's the cornerstone of the swing, the first building block on which everything else will eventually rest. If you turn out to be a talented golfer with some degree of athletic skill and an aptitude for hard work, you could reach a point where you're swinging the club at around 100 miles per hour at the moment of impact. During that swing the face of the club is rolling open and rolling back to a square position, your weight is shifting, your shoulders are turning, and your arms are rising and falling, all in an attempt to maximize clubhead speed and minimize the angle of the club face at that nanosecond when club meets ball. If you think you can control all those variables with any old grip you choose, you're fooling yourself.

A good grip allows both your hands to work as a single unit with maximum control and minimum pressure. If you're holding the club properly, you don't have to squeeze the life out of it to control where it's going. A good grip allows you to keep the pressure in your hands light without fear of the club slipping or dropping or falling. Because of that fact, working on a good grip from the beginning eliminates a lot of potential problems in your swing.

It's Not Natural

The problem with a good grip is that it feels awkward and unnatural in the beginning. When I teach beginners and I put their hands on the club correctly, the first words out of their mouths are, "Wow, that feels funny!"

I say, "Yes, but you have to work at it, because it's right and it's important." I know it feels strange.

Good players have a similar reaction when I try to change their grips. Frank Lickliter, one of the many PGA Tour players who lives in Ponte Vedra and practices at the TPC at Sawgrass, changed his grip slightly before the 2002 season. He called it "the toughest change" he's ever tried to make, but a critical one to the future of his game. Frank needed to learn to turn the ball in both directions—left and right—with every club in his bag. In order to do that, he had to modify the First Fundamental, a change that was like replacing the steel frame of a completed building.

If you think the grip seems unnatural to you, imagine how it must have felt to players like Harry Vardon, the guy who, through trial and error, invented what we consider the modern grip. At least those of us learning golf today have the benefit of 100 years of prior experiences from players like Vardon, Bobby Jones, Ben Hogan, Babe Zaharias, and Patty Berg. Those players developed their own grips by hitting thousands of balls and finding what worked. We have the benefit of their discoveries at our disposal. It's right in front of us if we're disciplined enough to follow their instructions.

The Left Hand

I teach students to place their left hands on the club first. For a right-handed player (which encompasses over ninety percent of the golfing population) the left arm is the "lead" arm—the arm that "leads" the club through the swing—so the left hand is the hand I want students to focus on first.

Standing erect with your left arm hanging naturally at your side, grip the club in your left hand so that the clubhead rests flat on the ground. Hold the club in your fingers, not your palm, and point your thumb down the grip. If you did this without twisting or manipulating your hand, you should be able to look down and see the knuckles of the first three fingers of your left hand.

Unfortunately, most people turn their hands when they grip a club so that their thumbs are directly on top of the grip, and they can't see the backs of their hands. That's wrong, and unnatural. If you stand in front of a mirror and let your arms hang in a relaxed position at your sides, the palms of your hands are going to point toward your hips. If you look down from this relaxed position, you can see the backs of your hands. It's only when we stand at attention and stiffen our arms that our hands rotate and the palms face our sides. It's from this rigid, unnatural position that most people grip a club for the first time.

All golfers, but particularly women, should put their left hands on the club with the back of the hand more on top of the club. This moves your thumb over to the right side of the grip rather than directly on top, and it allows you to see the knuckles of your index, middle, and ring finger.

This is a little different from the classic "palms facing" grip taught by players like Ben Hogan and Jack Nicklaus. The left-hand grip I teach my female students would have been considered a "strong" grip twenty years ago, but throughout the years I've seen too many women stick with weaker "palms facing" grips, even though their hands and arms aren't strong enough to swing the club from that position.

One of the biggest differences in the way I teach men and the way I teach women is the position of the left hand on the club. Because women, in general, lack hand strength, I always want women to err on the side of a stronger left hand.

I also find that my female students tend to let the club ride up into the palms of their hands more readily than do men. This creates a lot of long-term problems not only with their swings, but also with the blisters they rub on their hands. The club should run diagonally across the hand from the first knuckle of your left index finger to the base of the pad of your hand.

That sounds complicated, but there is a simple test to determine if you're gripping the club properly. Grip the club in your left hand, then

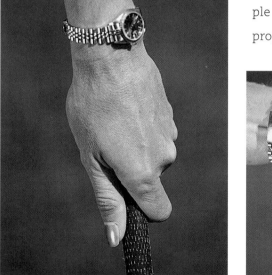

▼
The back of the left hand is more on top (note the three visible knuckles) and the butt of the grip rests against the pad of the hand.

straighten your middle finger, your ring finger, and your pinkie so that only your index finger is holding the club. Now pick the club up off the ground, balancing it between your index finger and the pad of your left hand. That's where the club should be in your hand. When you close the rest of your fingers, the club still should rest comfortably in that diagonal position.

The Reason for the Strong Left Hand

T he next question all my students ask is, "Why?" Why is it so important that the left hand be placed on the club in this manner? Since I've gone to great lengths to put your left hand in such a convoluted position on the golf club, the least I can do is explain what results you can expect.

In the golf swing, your wrists hinge on the backswing and unhinge on the downswing, creating clubhead speed at the moment of impact. The strong left hand enables you to set and release the club for maximum speed. It also allows you to control the club at the top of the backswing. A weaker grip can allow the club to flop at the top, but with the stronger grip, your left thumb keeps the club in the correct position.

Today the strong left hand is a mainstay among some of the greatest players in the world. David Duval's left hand would have been considered amateurishly strong a generation ago. Now it's a staple of the modern golf swing. Even players like Nicklaus have come around. After turning fifty and realizing the overpowering swing that allowed him to win eighteen professional majors wasn't the same with a fifty-year-old body and today's high-tech equipment, Nicklaus strengthened his left hand as part of a swing change that allowed him to compete for another decade as a senior.

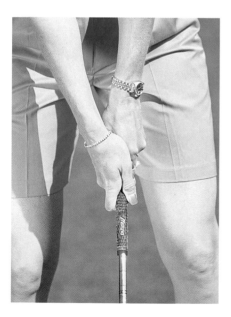

Right-hand Options

There are three ways to place the right hand on the club, but all of them start from a similar position. With your left hand on the club in the way previously described, you should place the palm of your right hand against your left thumb and close your hand around the club so that your left thumb rests comfortably in the nook between the pad and palm of your right hand. Your right thumb should be straight down the top of the golf club, and the crease,

▲

The three most
common golf grips:
Ten-finger, interlock-
ing, overlapping (or
Vardon) grip.

or V, formed between your thumb and hand should point toward your
sternum or your right breast.

Now you have all ten fingers on the golf club. You can choose to
stick with this grip if it feels comfortable and works for you. It's known
as a ten-finger grip and it's perfectly acceptable. Players like Bob Estes
have won numerous professional events gripping the club with all ten
fingers, and two-time LPGA Teacher of the Year Carol Preisinger has
played with a ten-finger grip her entire career. I recommend the ten-
finger grip to players who have great eye-hand coordination, but who
also have small, weak hands. If you fall into that category, you should
give the ten-finger grip a try. Otherwise, you might want to try the two
most popular grips in the game.

The first is called the interlocking grip, which as the name
implies, involves interlocking a couple of your fingers. To get the feel of
the interlocking grip, start out with the ten-finger grip as I've previously described, then interlock the pinkie of your right hand with the

► "A Tale of Two Grips"

- -

It was 1962 when a talented young lady from St. Louis named Judy Rankin made her debut on the LPGA Tour. Judy was young and full of promise, having become the youngest low amateur in the history of the U.S. Women's Open at age fifteen and the winner of the Missouri Amateur at age seventeen.

But at age eighteen and fresh out on tour, Judy came under immediate fire. Her left hand was too strong, many said. She couldn't play with her hand so far on top of the golf club. It defied every fundamental the pros of the time knew to be true.

Judy didn't listen to them. She knew that her hand position worked for her, and that was all that mattered. Twenty-six victories and one Hall of Fame induction ceremony later, Judy is considered a pioneer of the strong left hand grip, and a lot of players have been highly successful following her lead.

Not all old-school teaching professionals believed that a neutral, palms-facing grip was the way to go. In 1975 seventeen-year-old Hal Sutton trekked to Austin, Texas to take a lesson from renowned teacher

index finger of your left hand. You'll feel your hands move a little closer together as you interlock your fingers, and you'll find that your hands feel more stable on the club. Tiger Woods, Jack Nicklaus, and Nancy Lopez all use this interlocking grip—not bad role models if you're looking for pros to emulate.

But interlocking is not the most popular way to grip the club. The vast majority of professionals and amateurs use something called the overlapping grip, which is the grip Harry Vardon invented in the late 1800s. Players like Phil Mickelson, Karrie Webb, David Duval, and

- -

Harvey Penick, the soft-spoken guru responsible for teaching Ben Crenshaw and Tom Kite, among others. Penick was a legend, and the impressionable young Sutton couldn't wait to hear what he had to say.

"He said, 'I want you to hit your driver with no glove and I don't want you to practice or warm up,'" Sutton recalled. "I did what he said. I hit the first two or three not too good, and I hit the last two pretty good. Then he said, 'Now put your glove on and go through the normal routine.' I did that and hit about fifty balls without him saying a word. After that he said, 'Come over here and sit on the car and I want to show you a couple of things.' He stood up and said, 'There will be people who tell you your grip is too strong, but it's not. Don't worry about that.'"

Penick was right. Sutton arrived on tour in 1982 and was instantly criticized for his strong grip. The critics quieted down when Sutton won the Walt Disney World Classic in his rookie year and won the Players Championship and the PGA Championship his second year on tour. Twenty years after his first professional victory and twenty-seven years after that fateful lesson with Harvey Penick, Sutton still hasn't changed his strong left-hand grip. And he's still winning golf tournaments.

Se Ri Pak, as well as seventy-five percent of the general golfing population use this grip. It's similar to the interlocking grip, but as the name implies, the fingers overlap rather than interlock. The pinkie of your right hand rests in the crevice between the index and middle finger of your left hand. That leaves all five fingers of your left hand firmly on the club, and gives you a greater sense of control with your left hand.

Which Grip
Is Right for You?

Picking a grip is a matter of personal preference. The old rule of thumb used to be that players with weak or small hands needed to use the ten-finger or interlocking grip and players with larger, stronger hands overlapped. That isn't a firm and fast rule. Bob Estes has strong hands, and he uses the ten-finger grip, and nobody has ever accused Tiger Woods of having weak or small hands and he interlocks. I used to interlock, but with my long fingers and strong hands, I found that the club rode up into my palms too easily and I wasn't hinging my wrists properly, so, in the middle of a golf tournament, I switched to the overlapping grip. While I don't recommend such a radical change during the middle of a competition, the move was right for me, and I've never regretted making it.

You should experiment with different grips until you find one that feels comfortable. Also, ask your teaching pro for advice. A competent professional can evaluate your grip and make sound recommendations based on your strength, size, and eye-hand coordination.

Don't Be Afraid to Change

When I'm teaching intermediate and good players, the most hostile responses I get come when I suggest a grip change. That's because good players know minor grip adjustments can lead to months of poor shotmaking.

All changes take time. It doesn't matter what adjustment you attempt to make in your swing, you're probably going to hit it worse before you hit it better. That's the nature of the game.

Changing your grip is hard. A minor change will initially cause you to hit it sideways. But if you trust your teacher, and if you believe that a grip change is necessary for your long-term success, bite the bullet, make the change, and work your way through the bad patch. It's hard, but it will ultimately be worth it.

Strengthening the Hands

Women generally have weaker hands and forearms than men, but that doesn't mean you can't work on improving your strength in these areas. Because I played softball and basketball for years before I took up golf, my hand and arm strength was good for a woman my size. But once I started working on my golf game I realized how much stronger I needed to be in those areas if I wanted to compete at the highest level. Through hard work, I've gotten much stronger in my hands and forearms. Today I have stronger hands than most of the men I teach, a point I never make during the lessons but one I'm proud of.

Three of the exercises I used to get stronger and ones I recommend to all my female students are:

■ *Squeezing a ball.* Use a ball that is soft enough to squeeze but still provides some resistance. Holding the ball as if it were the enlarged grip of a golf club, squeeze and release it fifty times with each hand, then rest for a couple of minutes before repeating the exercise. I recommend three or four sets of fifty squeezes with each hand. It might take a while for you to work up to that level, but once you make this exercise part of your daily routine, you'll by shocked how much stronger your hands become.

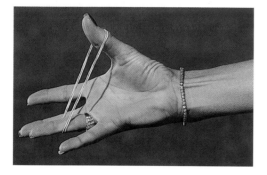

▲

Stretching a rubber band strengthens the hands and improves your game.

■ *Pulling rubber bands.* Where squeezing the ball works the muscles that contract the fist, this exercise strengthens the opposing muscles, those that allow you to open your hand. Simply wrap a rubber band around your thumb and one of your fingers, looping the band around a couple of times until your finger and thumb are reasonably close together. Then stretch the band by opening your hand as wide as possible. Repeat this exercise at least twenty times with each finger of both hands. Again, I'd like to see every student work up to three or four sets of twenty pulls with each finger, but that will take some time. The good news is if you work on this exercise every day for a week, you'll see immediate and dramatic changes in your hand strength.

■ *Slowly rotating a club.* Holding a golf club straight up with your arm outstretched, slowly lower the club ninety degrees to the left until it is parallel with the ground, then slowly rotate it back 180 degrees to the right until it is parallel with the ground on the other side. The key to this exercise is making your motion slow and deliberate. It should take you a full five or six seconds to rotate the club from one side to the other. If you repeat this exercise twenty to thirty times with each arm, your forearms will become much stronger.

Making It Second Nature

▲

Slowly rotate a club from noon to nine and three o'clock to strengthen your hands and forearms for golf.

I have a 5-iron conveniently located by the couch in my living room, and I always keep a wedge or two in various corners of my kitchen or bedroom. This isn't because I'm a lousy housekeeper; I keep these clubs handy so I can practice my grip while I'm watching television or waiting on the microwave to announce that my popcorn is ready.

You should keep a club or two around the house for the same reason. The golf grip isn't natural. But with practice, your grip will become second nature to you. When that happens, you can feel confident that you are building your golf swing on a solid bedrock.

ONCE YOU HAVE YOUR HANDS on the golf club, you need to get your body into position to strike the ball. It is at this stage that a lot of women enter lockdown mode—the place where muscles become rigid, minds get cluttered, and the concept of relaxation is lost. You've seen it dozens of times as golfers go through their mental checklists: left arm straight, head down, chin up, bottom out, right arm tucked, left foot angled, knees flexed, eyes on the ball. By the time these people tick off all the things they're supposed to remember, they're frozen in space like some contorted bronze statue. Swinging a club from this unpliant position is tough. Hitting a good golf shot is impossible.

6 The Setup

That's why I teach students to think of their setups in terms of results, not process. Your goal in golf is to swing the club as fast and efficiently as possible in order to move the ball from one spot to another (hopefully a spot closer to the hole). The setup is the position of your body, the ball, and the club that maximizes your chances of reaching that objective. If someone tells you to tie yourself in knots in order to set up properly, an alarm should go off in your head, and you should say to yourself, "Wait a minute. How can I make a fast, efficient swing from this position? I can barely move! And what good is this list of things I'm supposed to remember if I'm too tense to swing the club?"

If you keep your eye on the objective—moving the ball from point A to point B—you have a pretty good shot at improving your setup.

Why Is It So Hard?

I like to draw comparisons between the posture you assume for golf and the setup for other sporting activities like shooting a free throw in basketball or preparing to return a serve in tennis or getting ready to play defense in soccer. My teacher, Ed Oldfield, told me to set up as though I were about to defend a fast point guard with a great jump shot. That was something I understood, so getting my body in that position was easy.

Your posture to hit a golf ball isn't much different than the position you assume to play defense, shoot a shot, catch a ball, or return a serve. No matter what sport you're playing, your feet have to be about shoulder-width apart so that your weight is evenly distributed. From that position you are in balance and you have the ability to move. Your back is fairly straight; your shoulders aren't hunched or slumped; you're slightly bent at the waist; and your hands and arms are in front of your body. This is the posture a basketball coach will tell you to get in at the foul line and the one a tennis pro will put you in to hit a ground stroke. A soccer coach will tell her team to get in that position to play defense, and a softball manager will recommend that posture to a shortstop fielding ground balls. It's a universal athletic posture, one from which all sporting activities take place.

So why is it so hard to replicate that posture when you have a golf club in your hands? The answer is simple: golf is a static sport. In basketball, softball, tennis, soccer, field hockey, and cricket you are reacting to other movement. The ball is coming at you, or other players are running toward you. You're probably winded and tired, filled with adrenaline from the activity and excitement of the game. You don't have a lot of time to think, and you certainly don't have the where-withal to go through a mental checklist that includes where your feet are positioned and whether or not your back is straight. If you ponder those things, even for a second, the game will pass you.

Golf is different. The ball is sitting still, and you, the golfer, have all the time in the world to contemplate where, when, and how you're going to grip the club, line up, address the ball, and swing. Instructors often call this deliberative process "paralysis by analysis," the rigor mortis that sets in when you overanalyze every particular of your setup. By the time you're ready to swing the club, you're frozen in place with no chance of generating any swing speed or control.

Perfect Posture

Just as in putting, the perfect posture for striking the golf ball is an athletic position from which you can move with agility while maintaining your balance. Your feet are shoulder-width apart on average—a little wider for your longest clubs and a little narrower for your shortest shots, but nothing dramatic either way—and your knees are slightly flexed, a position you might assume if you were about to catch a basketball being thrown in your direction.

From that base, you bend your body forward, hinging from your hips so that your back is straight and your shoulders don't sag. This requires you to feel like you are sticking your bottom out and pointing your chest at the ball, so you can't be inhibited. The fact is a good golf posture isn't lewd or exhibitionist. A good setup feels awkward, but it looks great. Just look at players such as Annika Sorenstam and Se Ri

Pak as examples. Their posture is perfect, and nobody has ever accused
either of them of indecency.

Too many women shy away from this position for fear that they're
creating some sort of spectacle, when exactly the opposite is true. The
golfers who draw the most unwarranted attention to themselves are
the ones who set up with their rears drawn underneath them or with
their knees so flexed that they have no chance of making a comfortable swing. These setups aren't very comfortable, and they're terrible
for your game.

Good posture sends a signal to those around you that you are
serious about your game. It's worth spending the extra time in front of
a mirror to get this part of the setup mastered.

What Sport Can You Name That You Play on Your Heels?

T hat was one of the first questions my teacher asked me when I was learning the proper posture for the golf swing, and it's the one I ask all my students now. Can you name a sport you play with all your weight on your heels? I can't. For all sports, from croquet to cricket, ping pong to polo, the player who sets up with her weight on her heels is the one who's going to have trouble. These games are played from the balls of your feet, a spot where you can move freely while remaining balanced. Golf is no different.

Good golf is played with the weight evenly distributed throughout your feet. The best way to insure this posture is to keep your kneecaps directly over the center of your feet. If your knees extend beyond your feet, your weight is too far forward and into your toes. When you swing the club, the force of the swing will pull you forward and you will have to catch your balance by moving your feet. If your knees are locked or over your ankles, your weight is on your heels and you won't be able to make an effective turn. Only when your weight is evenly distributed on the balls of your feet are you in a position to make a great golf swing.

Throw the Stool Away

One of the oldest tips on the books, and one I would like to permanently abolish, says that you should set up to a golf ball as though you are sitting on a stool. That's awful advice. Invariably when I see people with poor setups—weight on their heels, shoulders slumped, butt tucked underneath them—my first question is, "What are you thinking about when you set up?"

More often than not, "Sitting on a stool" is the answer I get.

Forget it. Chess is the only game I've seen played from a stool. Despite the great shots you might see from some trick-shot artists, the golf swing requires a freedom of motion you can't gain sitting down. If you're one of the many golfers who has heard the "Sit on a stool" axiom, try to erase it from your memory. You'll make better swings if you do.

Freedom to Swing

Perfect posture allows your arms to hang freely, which is critical to making a good golf swing. If, from this position, you relax your arms and sway your body from side to side, your arms should swing back and forth like ropes hung from a tree. That is the golf swing in miniature. Your arms are like the ropes of a swing with the golf club being the chair. If you've ever sat in a swing, you know that the fastest moment in the swinging cycle is when the chair is closest to the ground and the forces of gravity and momentum are at their peaks. But you also know that any tension in the ropes—a knot or a tree limb getting in the way, for example—will break the rhythm and

slow the chair. In order for you to swing fast and high, the ropes must be loose and unencumbered.

The same principle applies in golf. In order for you to swing the golf club properly, your arms must be free to move without tension. A good, athletic posture accomplishes that goal.

The K Club

. . . .

Now grip the club, and you'll notice something interesting. Your right hand is lower than your left (for a right-handed player), and unless your arms are of differing lengths, your right shoulder drops slightly lower than your left shoulder. Looking at yourself in a full-length mirror, you can almost imagine your body as the letter K,

◄

With both hands on the
club your body should
form a reverse K.

with your left side being the straight-line side of the K and the right
side providing the letter's arm and leg.

You have to be somewhat imaginative to visualize this K phenomenon, but this setup key puts you in a good position from which to
swing the club.

The Breast Question

Every woman golfer wants to know how their breasts affect their
setup, but few, if any, ever ask the question. That's understandable. It's not a conversation you want to have with the young
assistant or old teaching pro at your club. Still, the well endowed
among us need to know what to do with the darned things.

At the sake of simplifying something that can get quite complicated, my general rule of thumb is, left arm on top of the left breast, and right arm underneath the right breast. This puts you in the perfect K position. Now, for some smaller women, this might not be appropriate, and for the largest among us it might be impossible. But for the vast majority of women this is a quick and simple answer you've always wanted to know but were afraid to ask.

Heads Up

One of the most frequently uttered "tips" amateurs offer to their friends and playing partners is the old "Keep your head down" saw. You've probably heard husbands sharing this little tidbit of wisdom with their wives (in a less-than-subtle too-loud voice on most occasions), and you might even have been on the receiving end of a "Keep your head down" comment or two yourself.

The problem with this tip is it's not only wrong, it's terrible for your posture. All good golf swings require balance, and one of the best ways to maintain that balance is to build your swing around a relatively still head. But "Keep your head still or steady" is quite a bit different than "Keep your head down."

Too many players, particularly women, take the advice to heart. I see them on the practice tee every day with their chins on their chests, awkwardly swatting at balls with no concept of the damage they are doing to their games. When I tell these players that they should lift their chins and keep their heads up, they can't believe it. "Everybody tells me to keep my head down," they say.

"Has it worked?" I ask.

"Well, no."

"Okay then, try it my way and let's see if you notice a difference."

They always do. Your shoulders and arms have to have room to turn freely during the golf swing. You can't make that turn if your chin is in the way.

I always tell my students that if they cannot comfortably place a fist underneath their chins, they're dropping their heads too much. That's a good rule of thumb for all golfers.

After setting up, take your right fist and place it under your chin. If you can do so easily while keeping your eyes on the ground where the clubhead should be, then your spine should be reasonably straight and you should have plenty of room to turn during the swing. If you can't fit your fist under your chin, you need to work on keeping your head up, not down.

I tell my students that until they master the setup, they shouldn't bother swinging the club. It is the most important of all fundamentals.

▲

Place a fist under your chin to make sure your head and neck are in the right position.

Some ways to work on your setup include:

- *Set up in front of a mirror.* Repetition is the key to success, but in order to repeat a good setup position, you have to know what your setup looks like. That's why I tell my students to spend time in front of a full-length mirror working on their setups. Once you see how you look, you can compare your setup with that of other good players. Only then can you grow comfortable with a good, balanced setup.

- *Swing on a balance beam or a workout ball.* For my more advanced students, I recommend a couple of balance drills to insure good posture and setup. The first is to swing while standing on a balance beam, not one that's suspended off the ground, but a four-by-four

▶ CINDY'S INTERMEDIATE TIP

The Importance of Setup

- -

When asked to rank the most important aspects of golf, Jack Nicklaus said he considered the setup to be eighty percent of the game, and the swing to be only twenty percent. "You can hit a decent shot with a good setup and a marginal swing," Jack said. "But you can have a great swing and poor setup and never hit a good shot."

Jack's not alone. Ben Hogan thought that setup was the most crucial fundamental in golf, and Tiger Woods considers it "a critical basic" for all good golf. When Annika Sorenstam was working on her record-setting 2001 season on the LPGA Tour, she cited an improved and "more comfortable" setup as one of the key elements in her success.

If all these great players put that much emphasis on setup, doesn't it make sense that amateurs should spend much of their practice time refining the setup?

- -

lying in your garage or basement. Any mistakes in your setup you might have gotten away with on the golf course will be magnified on the balance beam.

Once you're comfortable swinging on the balance beam, you should progress to the inflatable workout ball, the kind gym instructors suggest for crunches and lateral-oblique lifts. Only I want you to stand on the ball and swing a golf club. Just standing on the thing takes some time and effort. You have to start on your knees, then progress to a squatting position, before you can stand on this type of ball. But once you are erect, there's nothing better for your game than making swings while standing on one of these balls.

This is the most advanced setup and balance drill. Four-time national long drive champion Jason Zubak actually hits balls while standing on one of these balls. I would never recommend that to anyone, but slowly working on your balance until you are able to stand and swing on a workout ball is the best drill imaginable for insuring a good, consistent, balanced setup.

Ball Position

B ecause the golf ball is sitting still, golfers have the luxury of deciding where to position the ball relative to their bodies. This can be either a blessing or a curse. We don't have to worry about a pitcher throwing a curve ball at us, but on the other side, we have to make a good decision on where to place the ball for maximum distance and accuracy.

There are two schools of thought on ball position. The first theory is that the ball should always be played in the same spot in your stance no matter what club you're swinging. Typically this position is just inside the heel of your left foot. Players like Nancy Lopez and Karrie Webb play all their shots from this position and do quite well.

The other theory, the one I subscribe to and teach to most of my students, is a sliding position where the ball is played off the left heel for the longer clubs, like woods and long irons, but played progressively closer to the middle of the stance as the clubs get shorter. I believe in playing the ball in the middle of your stance when you're hitting a wedge, and off your left (or front) foot when you're hitting a driver. All other clubs are played somewhere in between those two positions depending on the length of the club and the type of shot you're trying to hit.

Tiger Woods positions the ball this way, as does Annika Sorenstam and Se Ri Pak, not bad players to emulate if you're looking to copy someone's technique.

The best way to determine your personal ball position preference is to alternate clubs in practice, much as you would on the golf course. Hit one ball with the driver; then hit your next practice shot with an 8-iron. Your third shot should be played with a 3-iron and your fourth with a wedge. Pay attention to the relative position of the ball in your stance on each of these swings and take note of the differences. If you're playing your wedge in the same spot in your stance as your driver, pay attention to the ball flight and the feel of the hit for each shot. Chances are that one or the other felt good, but not both. Since I can't be with you on every shot you hit, only through trial and error will you get comfortable with where to play the ball in your stance.

One of the most asked questions I get about ball position is "How far away from the ball should I stand?" Unfortunately there's no answer I can give to that question that satisfies everyone. Tall thin people with long arms will stand farther away from the ball than will short stocky people with stubby arms.

The drill I prescribe for my students who are struggling with ball position is to stand erect and extend your arms straight out in front of you so that the club is pointing to the sky. Then establish your setup position, setting your feet shoulder-width apart and bowing at the waist as you would if you were about to swing the club. Now let the club-head drop to the ground.

Wherever the club hits the ground is how far away from it you should stand.

Some players reach too far for the ball, causing their swings to be too flat. The club never gets above their shoulders on the backswing, and the angle of the swing is too shallow as they approach impact. This often leads to pushed, pulled, topped, and even shanked shots. It's hard to tell someone who has just shanked a shot to stand closer to the ball at address, but in most cases that's what needs to happen. By standing a little closer to it, your arms hang closer to your body and

▶

Ball forward with
driver, ball centered
with 6-iron, ball back
with wedge.

◄

When the arms fall
naturally, the eyes are
over the hands. This
is the perfect spot to
play the ball.

your swing becomes more upright. This allows for more solid strikes with less variance in clubface angle.

You can get too close to it, though. If you're standing so close to the ball that your arms cannot swing past your body, you will likely compensate by picking up the club with your hands. Once you've picked up the club with your hands, you have no chance of making solid contact. You will throw the club at the ball. If you make contact at all, it won't be pretty.

I believe that in the perfect setup your eyes are directly over your hands. That might vary a few inches depending on the length of your arms or how tall you are, but it's a good rule of thumb. If you're having trouble establishing ball position, try setting up, then take one hand off the club and drop a ball from your left eye. If the ball hits the hand you still have on the club, you're in pretty good shape. If not, try adjusting your hand position.

Alignment: The Most Important Fundamental

I f, as Jack Nicklaus has said, setup constitutes eighty percent of golf's fundamentals, then alignment has to make up at least seventy-five to eighty percent of the setup in terms of overall importance. Lining up correctly is the most critical fundamental in golf. If you set up with your body and the club aligned toward the target, you can mishit your shot (sometimes badly) and still advance the ball toward the hole and end up with a reasonably good result. I've even seen players make holes-in-one with shots they didn't hit very well, but the balls found the hole anyway because they were lined up correctly.

If you don't line up toward the hole, then the greatest golf swing in the world isn't going to produce the results you want. In fact, if you're lined up wrong, you actually have to make a bad swing in order to push, pull, hook, or slice the ball toward your intended target.

Finding the Line

T o fully understand alignment, you must first grasp the concept of "target line." It should be simple. The target line is an imaginary line between the ball and the target. In order to advance the ball along that imaginary line, you have to align your feet, hips, and shoulders on a line parallel to the target line and you have to put the clubhead behind the ball so that the clubface is pointing toward the target.

This seems like a simple concept, one that is both logical and

intuitive. If you want the ball to travel along a particular line, you have to align your body and the club along that same line. But a lot of players, particularly women, have a great deal of trouble understanding and finding the target line.

I see it every day. A woman stands on the range hitting balls twenty, thirty, sometimes forty yards off-line. She checks her swing, goes through her mental checklist for setting up, but never once looks at her alignment. When I mention that she could correct her problem by aligning her body along the target line, the woman looks at me like I have two heads. Then I put clubs on the ground to show the student her target line.

"Wow, that feels awkward," she says. This is an almost universal reaction from my female students. They can't believe their alignment could be as much as ten to twenty degrees off-line, but in some cases it's even worse than that.

▲
A closed stance
(aimed right of target);
an open stance
(aimed left of target);
a "square" stance
(aimed straight at target).

Check Alignment by Placing Clubs on the Ground

All players need to check their alignment occasionally. One of the biggest differences between good players and intermediate or so-so players is the frequency with which they check their alignment. Good players check their alignment all the time. Average players don't check it often enough.

The best way to check alignment is to place two clubs on the ground so that the grips of the clubs are pointing toward the target. You then align your feet, hips, and shoulders in a line parallel with those clubs.

Go to any LPGA event and you'll see half the players on the range practicing with clubs on the ground marking their alignment. At your local club, you'll be fortunate to find one player practicing with clubs on the ground. That, in a nutshell, is the difference.

Always Start from Behind the Ball

Practicing with these clubs positioned on the ground conditions your mind and body to the feeling of lining up toward your intended target. But you can't lay clubs on the ground on the golf course. You have to devise a way to find your target line without those visual aids, and as any professional will tell you, the simplest and best way to accomplish that goal is to start every shot from behind the ball. Standing on the target line behind the ball allows you to visualize the line in your mind. Some players even draw an imaginary ribbon or rainbow from the ball to the target. The mental cue you use is a personal preference. The objective is to find the target line and keep that line in your mind as you walk up to the ball and go through your setup.

Laura Diaz, one of the best and brightest young players on the LPGA Tour today, stands behind every shot and points the club down the target line as she's setting her grip. This gives her a mental image of the target line, one she carries through the rest of her routine and into her setup and swing.

Jack Nicklaus and Greg Norman pick out a spot on the ground, a blade of grass or an indentation a few feet in front of their balls along the target line, and they use those spots as visual cues to help them align their bodies. Other players, like Lori Kane, draw imaginary lines through the ball toward the hole and line up on the dimples in the ball

▼

Always start from behind the ball to pick your line.

Don't Put a Club to Your Hips

I was playing with one of my students not long ago when, after hitting an off-line shot, she put a club to her hips and attempted to look down the line of the club to see what might have gone awry.

"What are you doing?" I asked.

"Seeing if my hips were lined up wrong," she answered.

"No, you're not," I said. "To begin with, you can't tell anything by putting a club to your hips after the fact. If you put a club on the ground at your feet immediately after a shot you can tell how your feet were lined up. But you can change the alignment of your hips without moving anything else on your body. Your hips move throughout the swing anyway. You're wasting your time putting that club to your hips."

I didn't tell her she was also sending a signal to anyone watching that she didn't know anything about golf. Nothing signals "novice" faster than putting a club to your hips to check your alignment. It's irrelevant, useless, and a practice you need to avoid.

that this line bisects. I extend my imaginary line to the edge of my peripheral vision. This keeps me conscious of the path I want the club to travel during the swing as well as insuring that I line up properly.

Whatever mental and visualization tool you choose, always starting the process from behind the ball will help put you in the right spot at address.

Give Your Setup
the Time It Deserves

- -

If alignment is the most important part of the setup, and the setup is the most important fundamental in golf, it stands to reason that you should practice alignment and setup more than anything else in the game. Unfortunately, most people spend very little time working on their setups and even less time checking their aim and alignment.

Don't fall into that trap. Spend time at home in front of a mirror working on setting up properly and getting comfortable in a good golf posture. Then spend time on the driving range with clubs on the ground to insure your ball position and alignment are correct. It's time well spent, as you will see from the results on the course.

WOULDN'T IT BE GREAT if you could hit every single fairway with your drives and find every green with your approach shots? Finding fourteen fairways and eighteen greens a round would be a dream come true. Unfortunately, that's all it is: a dream. The best players in the world miss fairways and greens, and sometimes they miss a lot of them. Annika Sorenstam only hit seventy-eight percent of the fairways and greens in 2001, the year she shattered the LPGA season-long scoring record and won Player of the Year honors. Tiger Woods hit only seventy percent of the fairways and seventy-two percent of the greens that same year when he won five PGA Tour events and earned his third straight Player of the Year title.

7 Scoring Shots

The difference between players who consistently shoot good scores and those who hit the ball well but shoot scores that are higher than they would like is the ability to recover when they miss fairways and greens. Good players make pars on the twenty or thirty percent of the holes where they miss the fairway or the green. Mediocre players turn those misses into bogeys or double bogeys.

I was lucky. When I started this game, I couldn't afford to hit 500 balls a day because range balls cost $5 a bag, and I couldn't spend $30 a day on practice balls. But that didn't mean I couldn't practice. In the mornings I would buy a bag of range balls and hit chip shots, pitch shots, and bunker shots for a couple of hours, then go to the range and hit the balls away. I would repeat that process after lunch, and do it once more in the evening. Pretty soon I learned to stretch three bags of range balls into a ten-hour day in the practice area. I also developed a deft short game that served me well when I made my foray onto the course.

I learned this lesson by accident. You don't have to. Low scores don't come from long drives or long, crisp iron shots. If they did John Daly and Laura Davies would win every week on the professional tours. Golfers are not robots. We're going to miss some shots. We're going to miss fairways, and we're going to miss greens. We're going to hit shots that we think are perfect until a gust of wind knocks the ball into a greenside bunker, and we're going to hit some not-so-perfect shots that leave us in spots on the course we didn't know existed. The mark of a good player is how she recovers from those precarious predicaments, how she plays the "scoring shots," and how many times she snatches par from the jaws of a double bogey.

The scoring shots come in all shapes and sizes. There's the straightforward pitch or chip, the sand shot and the lob shot, all of which are needed at least once a round for most players. Then there are the more testy shots, the ones where the ball is nestled in the high grass on a hillside below your feet. These shots require you to be imaginative, innovative, and confident in your abilities.

They also require you to be realistic. I can't tell you the number of times I've seen players make double bogey or higher because they tried to play a recovery shot that Tiger Woods wouldn't have attempted. Part of playing the scoring shots is learning when to attempt an aggressive shot and when to play it safe. There are plenty of scoring opportunities in every round. It's up to you to recognize them when you see them and hit the shot that's appropriate for your situation.

Chips:
The Get-It-Close Shots

Missing the green with your approach shot doesn't mean you have to settle for an over-par score. In fact, I know a lot of players who feel just as comfortable standing over a twenty-foot chip shot as they would if they had a twenty-five-foot putt. They're just as likely to make it from the fringe as they are from the putting surface given the right conditions.

Chipping and putting have a lot of similarities. The swinging motion of both chips and putts is small and dictated by the shoulders and arms. The lower body remains still and steady on both chips and putts, and both the putter and the club you use for chipping should follow through on the line you wish the ball to travel. Another important similarity is distance control. Good chippers, like good putters, control the distances of their chip shots. Even their off-line chips don't roll too far from the hole.

So, how do they do it? How do good chippers build such deft touch and consistency around the greens? Is it a natural skill like singing or songwriting that is God-given? Or is it a learned craft? And most important, what can you do to become more like them?

The answer to those questions can only be found through hours of practice and a commitment to learning the art of the short game. But there are a few principles you should know before heading to the chipping area with your bag of balls.

Picking the Right Club

I n one of the classic old Warner Bros. film shorts where legendary golfer Bobby Jones is giving instruction to golfers of the 1930s, a young lad in knickers and a broadcloth shirt says, "Mr. Jones, do you always chip with a niblick [the hickory shaft equivalent of a wedge]?"

"Most certainly not," Jones says in his syrupy Southern drawl. "I often chip with a mashie-niblick or even a mashie. It is a mistake to try to make one club do for all kinds of chips. Always select a club with which you can pitch to the edge of the putting surface."

With that the boy in the film smiles, nods, and skips off to a better game. It was hokey, even by 1930s standards, but the golf principles the great Mr. Jones espoused were perfect back then and right on target to this day. One of the biggest mistakes I see among women golfers is the tendency to chip with a wedge no matter what the circumstances. This is just as wrong today as it was sixty years ago. Good chippers choose a club that will get the ball on the ground and rolling toward the hole as quickly as possible.

In my short-game clinics I often put my students in spots just off the green where I say, "Okay, you have to get up and down from here. But there's one catch. You can't use any of your wedges."

This is usually met with a lot of groans.

"Look," I say. "I'm being kind. When I was learning the short game from Seve Ballesteros, he gave me a 3-iron and made me get up and down from everywhere. I learned to be pretty imaginative with that 3-iron. I'm giving you eleven clubs to choose from. They just aren't the clubs you're accustomed to using."

▲

When you can,
carry the ball to the
edge of the putting
surface and let it roll
to the hole.

My students don't like this in the beginning, but by the end of the session, they are amazed by their own creativity. They're hitting bump shots, running chips, shots that get on the ground and roll to the hole, and shots that end up closer than they would have if they had been played with any of the wedges I've confiscated.

If you are faced with only a few feet of fringe to carry and a long section of green between the edge of the green and the hole, you should always take a less lofted club and fly the ball to the edge of the green. This requires a much smaller stroke than needed if you were trying to fly the ball all the way to the hole. It also offers you a chance to roll the ball like a putt rather than trying to fly the ball into the hole.

To illustrate the difference in rolling the ball to the hole and flying it to the hole, try a little experiment. Try throwing a ball underhanded from the edge of the green to the hole. Fly it as close as you can and measure how close it ends up to the cup. Now roll a ball from that same spot, pitching it to the edge of the green and letting it roll the remaining distance. Not only will the motion of your arm be a lot smaller for the second action, if you repeat that exercise four or five times, you will almost always roll the ball closer than you can pitch it.

You should take a club with enough loft to get the ball on the green and stop it near the hole. If the hole is cut close to the edge of the green where your ball is resting, you might want to use a wedge, sand wedge, or even a lob wedge, depending on how quickly you need to stop the ball. If, however, you have an ample amount of green between your ball and flag, try chipping with a 9-iron, 8-iron, 7-iron, or 6-iron. With a little work you'll be surprised how much closer you chip the ball to the hole.

▼

The ball is back in the stance.

Setting Up for Success

Because the chip shot doesn't require a full swing, you don't need a full-swing setup. What you do need is a comfortable setup with good posture, your feet slightly closer together than on a full swing, and all your weight preset on your left side. The chip stroke isn't a long swing, so you don't need to worry about weight transfer. In fact, if you do shift your weight on a chip, you probably will hit the ball two or three times farther than you intended.

Once the weight is forward, position the ball slightly back of center in your stance so that your hands are slightly ahead of the ball. This insures that you will hit the ball with a descending blow, catching it crisply and causing it to pop into the air for a short distance.

Small Strokes, Big Results

Another fatal flaw I see more with my women students than I do with men is the tendency to take a long, slow stroke for a shot that only travels a short distance. Sometimes my students take the club back so far on these short shots that I flinch, thinking that the ball is surely going to come screaming off the club right at my head. Even my intermediate and good-playing students make this mistake. It's as if they want to adjust the distance they hit the ball by adjusting the speed of their swings, not the length of their strokes. This is wrong, and it creates a lot of missed opportunities.

The best played chip shots are made with short strokes where the clubhead barely rises above ankle height and your hands never get any higher than your right hip. Both hands are passive in the well-played chip stroke, just as they are in a well-struck putt. Any attempt to scoop or lift the ball during the chip shot causes you to either hit behind the ball, chunking the club into the ground and moving the ball only a few inches, or you will hit the top of the ball and it will roll well past your intended target.

By keeping the hands passive and letting the left shoulder lead the chipping stroke, you improve your chances of hitting the shot exactly the right distance with the right amount of spin.

You also never see a good chipper stick the clubhead in the ground so that it stops immediately after impact. A well-played chip shot is like a well-struck putt. The follow-through is at least as long as the takeaway.

The chip-shot sequence goes something like this:

- **Envision the shot you want to hit.** See the shot in your mind before you play it. Pick the spot where the ball should fly to, the height the ball should fly to get there, the speed it should be going when it lands, and the amount of roll you expect.

- **Take a couple of practice strokes.** Keeping the image of the shot in your mind, take a couple of practice strokes to insure that you know how hard you should hit the ball to produce your desired results.

- **Set up with a slightly open, slightly narrower-than-normal stance.** This is a short swing. It requires a short motion, and therefore a shorter, more open stance.

- **Relax your hands.** No good chip shot was ever struck with the club in the throes of a death grip. Light grip pressure allows you to feel the shot, not force it.

- **Start the backswing with the left shoulder.** This is a pendulum stroke, similar to a putt. Therefore the stroke is initiated by pushing the club back with your left shoulder. Your arms and hands follow the shoulder's lead. The club moves back, but the hands and arms never venture too far from the body. Your shoulders are turning to produce this stroke.

▼

Note how soft and
passive my hands are
during this shot.

■   *Accelerate the club back to the ball smoothly.* There's no rush here. Granted, you shouldn't intentionally slow your swing to a snail's pace. You accelerate the downstroke in every swing. But you don't want to slap at the ball or stab the club in the ground because you get in too big of a hurry. Think smooth, not slow.

- **Hit down on the back of the ball.** Focus on one dimple if you have to, but pick a spot where you want to make contact with the ball and be sure to hit the ball on that spot.

- **Follow through to the target.** Let your follow-through follow the path you want the ball to travel. A good stroke does little good if you hit the ball off-line.

- **Watch closely as your ball rolls into the hole.**

Pitching: The Hit-It-Short-and-Stop-It-Quick Stroke

A lot of greens today are anything but flat, and many of them are surrounded by humps, bumps, mounds, and depressions that may or may not contain sand, high grass, or crushed stone among other nasty things. Sometimes you don't have to miss a green very far to find yourself facing a difficult little shot over such an obstacle. When that happens, you have to hit a pitch shot with one of your wedges.

The difference between a pitch and a chip, nomenclature that is often confused by even the best amateur players, is in the intended flight of the ball. A chip shot gets on the ground quickly and runs to the hole. A pitch shot flies high and short and stops on the green quickly. This is where having a good pitching wedge, sand wedge, and lob wedge is invaluable. These clubs are designed to loft the club in the air without any extraordinary effort on your part. The loft of the clubface is such that the ball jumps skyward when you make a smooth stroke.

The pitch stroke is slightly longer than the chipping motion. You should start the action by pushing the club back with your left side, initiating the pitch-shot motion with the left shoulder turning under your chin as the club moves away from the ball. Your stance is slightly narrower than shoulder-width. The ball is positioned in the middle of your stance, your weight is evenly distributed, and you might want to choke down on the grip of the club so that an inch or two of the grip is visible behind the pad of your left hand. This gives you greater control over the club, and cuts down on the tendency a lot of women have to slap at these shots with their hands.

Pretty quickly into the stroke, your wrists cock so that an L is formed between your left arm and the shaft of the club. This L is the hinge that will deliver the clubhead back to the ball squarely with the force necessary to hit the shot the desired distance. Your hands rarely go past waist high unless you have an extremely long distance to carry the ball. The club is delivered back to the ball by a firm (not stiff) left hand, arm, and side.

Your lower body is passive throughout the backswing. Your head remains reasonably still. The angle of your back is unchanged. You don't slump, lift, lunge, or sway your torso. This is simply a turning motion with the shoulders initiating the move, and the arms and hands lifting the club back and bringing it through.

When a student is having trouble understanding how this motion feels, I tell her to imagine slapping a pillow with the back of her left hand. Obviously your left wrist wouldn't break as you were slapping the pillow. Neither should it break when you're hitting a pitch shot. The left shoulder, arm, and hand lead the club down and through the shot.

This shot is, at its core, a miniature version of the full swing. As such there is some lower body action. Too many women attempt to hit pitch shots without moving their lower bodies at all. The results aren't pretty. Just as you can't make consistent solid contact in your full swing without your lower body turning through the shot, attempting to hit pitch shots with only your arms and upper body will produce low, screaming skulls or chunked chili-dips. Only when you turn your hips through the shot and finish with your belt buckle facing the target can you hit consistent, solid pitch shots.

With your lower body facing the target, the only thing left to do is finish the stroke. Just as is the case in putting and chipping, the follow-through for the pitch shot should be the same length as the backswing. This insures good rhythm throughout the stroke and keeps you consistent in every shot you play.

The pitch-shot sequence goes something like this:

■   *Choose the lofted club you need.* This is usually the sand wedge or the lob wedge, but occasionally the pitching wedge is the right call. It all depends on how high and far you need the ball to fly.

■   *Pick the spot on the green where you need to fly the ball.* If this means walking up the green and having a look, do it. Never hit a pitch shot without some idea of where you want the ball to fly to and what sort of result you can expect.

■   *Take a few practice swings focusing on your hands.* The hands play a more active role in the pitch shot, so you should take a little time getting the feel for setting your L and accelerating through the shot.

- *Open and narrow your stance.* Just like a chip.

- *Take it back slow.* Too many women doom their pitch shots by jerking the club back quickly and destroying any sense of timing and tempo they might have had in the rest of their games. The shot requires a slow takeaway. Make it so.

- *Keep still as the club accelerates through impact.* The biggest destroyer of good pitch shots is the natural urge to want to lift or help the shot into the air. I see women with great setups and takeaways straighten their backs, lift their heads, and try to urge the ball upward. It never works out that way. Keep your head still, your knees flexed, and the angle of your back intact throughout.

- *Let the club do the work.* The loft of the club will throw the ball in the air if you hit down and through the shot. That thought will go a long way toward improving your pitch shots.

- *Face the target.* Finish with your belt buckle and chest facing the target.

- *Enjoy the great shot you've just hit!*

Lob Shots: The Sky-High-Soft-Landing Stroke

There are some occasions when you need to hit shots that fly straight up in the air and land softly near the hole. If, for example, you find yourself in a depression where the green is well above you and the pin is cut close to the edge, you need to be able to lob the ball high and soft in the hopes that it will stop close.

For this shot, you need to take a slightly wider stance keeping your weight firmly planted on your left side. Since you aren't trying to hit the ball a long way, weight shift isn't something you need for this shot. Putting your weight on your left foot and keeping it there insures a solid base from which to execute this shot. It also keeps the angle of your swing a little steeper, which is crucial in hitting high shots.

The ball is positioned slightly forward in your stance, similar to the spot where you might play a 5-iron shot, and you should, once again, choke down on the grip for control. Now, open the clubface so that it faces the sky. Your clubface should look like a pancake on the ground.

This is a shocking sight. You're going to be convinced that you can't possibly hit a shot with the clubface this open, but not only is it possible, it feels great. With an effortless, slow, smooth swing of the arms the ball rockets skyward like a circus star shot out of a cannon.

Your hands are passive, which gives this swing a much rounder look than the motion you'd use for a pitch shot. It takes a lot of work to condition your body to take a full, slow, relaxed swing for such a short shot. But it is one you'll want to add to your shot list. By having this shot in your bag, you can think creatively and objectively about which shot works best for every up-and-down situation.

The sequence is like this:

- **Pick your spot and your shot.** Just as you would with a chip or a pitch.

- **Take a wide stance with your knees flexed and your weight on your front foot.** This shot requires solid footing. A firm base gets you off on the right foot.

- **Open your stance and open the clubface.** Align your feet left of the target and open the clubface until it looks like a pancake lying on the ground. This will take a little getting used to. But it's the best adjustment you'll ever make.

- **Relax your hands and take a deep breath.** This is a slow, relaxed motion. It requires passive hands and a calm demeanor. Twitches and jerks won't cut it with this shot.

- **Think slow, long, and easy.** Keep the hands passive and think about sliding the club underneath the ball through impact.

- **Follow through and trust the result.** Just as you did with your chip and pitch, follow through to the target and watch your result.

Flop Shots Are for Dummies

One of my dearest friends is former PGA Tour commissioner and current Senior PGA Tour player Deane Beman, who also happens to be an authority on the short game. Deane was never a long hitter, even when he was competing on tour against guys like Jack Nicklaus and Arnold Palmer. But Deane could, in Arnold's words, "get up and down from some of the most unbelievable places you've ever seen." That was his strength, and he played to that strength throughout his career.

Once when I was playing a round of golf with Deane, I missed a green with one of my approach shots, and in an attempt to hit a crowd-pleasing recovery shot, I laid the face of my sand wedge wide open, took a wider than normal stance, opened my shoulders and feet to the target line, and took a full swing, trying to slide the club under the ball throwing it straight up in the air and onto the green. This is called a "flop" shot in professional circles, and it's become all the rage in the last few years. Unfortunately, my flop shot worked too well. The club did, indeed, slide under the ball causing it to fly straight up in the air. It landed softly on the ground and stopped immediately, just as I had intended. Only it landed fifteen feet short of the green. I had hit the shot perfectly, but I had misjudged the distance. Rather than having a putt for par, I was still faced with a delicate chip shot to a closely cut flag.

"What are you doing?" Deane asked.

"I was trying to hit a flop shot close to the hole," I said, as if this sort of thing were an everyday occurrence.

"You should never try a shot like that unless you practice it at least a hundred times a day," he said. "The risks are too high for the results you're likely to gain."

Then Deane gave me a short-game lesson that I've never forgotten and one I've incorporated into my teaching. He said, "Too many players get too cute with short shots for no reason other than they've seen pros do it on television. Remember that a short shot, a pitch or a chip, is simply a miniature version of your full swing. If you apply the same principles to the short shots that you do to your long, full shots, you'll hit the ball closer to the hole more often than you will if you try to pull off a shot you rarely ever practice."

It seemed so simple. The rest of that round and for days following, I tried out Deane's theory. Every time I missed a green, rather than trying to manufacture a shot I hadn't fully developed, I hit the shot I knew. My swing for these chips and pitches was simply a smaller version of my regular swing, the same motion I teach my beginning students to make when getting accustomed to the full swing.

The results were incredible. I found that I hit more shots closer to the hole by simplifying my approach than I had in previous months when I'd tried to be daring and bold. Some of the shots weren't miraculous or spectacular. I wouldn't have received any Ooohs or Ahhhs from the network announcing crews. But I found that I wasn't making bogeys and double bogeys as often either. It was a simple, utilitarian approach, but it worked! I found that by simplifying my motion and repeating the action I had grooved in my full swing, I got up and down from around the greens more frequently than I had with any other approach.

A few months later another friend of mine, NBC analyst Johnny Miller, validated Deane's lesson. Johnny said, "My next book is going to be titled *Flop Shots Are for Dummies*. It's ridiculous how often players will take a straightforward pitch shot and try to turn it into something more complicated than what it is. I don't know if they just want to hit that high full flop shot because it looks cool or what, but I've seen more shots thrown away trying to play that shot than I've seen saved with it."

I still keep the flop shot in my repertoire in case of emergencies, but I only pull it out on rare occasions.

Sand Play: Having a Blast

Nothing in golf elicits more dread among women than the sinister sand trap. It's petrifying. I've seen women break out in hives at the thought of climbing into a bunker to extricate their balls. For some reason hitting a shot out of the sand causes more angst among women than does the rough, the trees, or even the water. I've actually seen women who hit their balls in a water hazard cheer, saying, "Great! At least I didn't go into that awful sand pit!"

That sort of goofy logic is common among the women golfers I encounter. It's not that these women don't understand that the penalty for going into water is greater than the fine they're facing for hitting it in a bunker; it's that they don't care. You could penalize them two, three, or even four strokes as long as they don't have to crawl into that dreaded sand hole and flail about like a kid on the beach.

Sand shouldn't be that intimidating. Granted, hitting a sand shot isn't as easy as a chip or pitch from a pristinely mown fairway, but it isn't a cause for anguish. Here are some keys to taking the trouble out of the trap.

- ***Set up for the lie.*** Before you set up to hit your recovery shot from the sand, you need to examine how the ball is resting in the sand. If you have a good lie—that is, if the ball is sitting on top of the sand— the setup is almost identical to the one you would use for the lob shot. The ball is slightly forward in your stance, and your weight is on your left side.

However, if the ball is plugged or partially buried in the sand (often called a "fried egg" in golf slang), you should move the ball back

▲

Different lies are
played differently.
Good lie: ball forward.
Buried lie: ball back.

to the middle of your stance. You should also close the clubface slightly so the leading edge of the clubhead can dig into the sand and pop the ball out.

■   *Pick your distance and draw an imaginary line in the sand.* Greenside bunker shots are called "blasts" or "explosion" shots because you don't actually hit the ball. The clubhead hits the sand first at a predetermined spot behind the ball. The force of the club traveling through the sand pops the ball out of the bunker (along with a fair amount of sand) and stops it on the green.

The amount of sand you take with these shots depends on how far you intend to hit the ball and how much spin you hope to impart on the shot. For a high shot out of a deep bunker that needs to stop quickly, I suggest picking a spot about two inches behind the ball and drawing an imaginary line in the sand on that spot. This is the spot where you want the club to enter the sand. For longer bunker shots where less spin is warranted, choose a spot in the sand an inch or so behind the ball.

After you've picked your spot in the sand, forget about the ball. Since you aren't going to hit the ball anyway it's best not to think about it.

- *Pick a target that's a little long.* Most women leave their bunker shots short. Some fail to advance the ball more than a few feet, which is why there is so much anxiety over playing out of the sand in the first place. Because of this tendency, I tell most of my students to pick a target a little beyond the hole and try to hit the ball there. A good rule of thumb is to focus on the top of the flag as your target rather than the spot on the green where you want the ball to land. This will get you comfortable flying the ball farther from the sand and, hopefully, eliminate some of your sand-phobia.

- *Hit down and through.* More than any other time in golf, the desire to scoop the ball with the hands and arms is almost overwhelming when you're in the bunker. For some inexplicable reason, the thought of leaving the ball in the sand trap carries such a stigma that players want to lift, scoop, and throw the ball out of the sand as quickly as possible. Unfortunately, just as is the case with chips and pitches, this scooping action causes the player to either hit too far behind the ball or catch the top of the ball cleanly. Either way, you aren't getting out of the bunker.

The motion to hit a sand shot isn't too different from the motion you use to hit a pitch shot, except that you are hitting sand instead of ball, and because you're hitting sand first, you're also taking a slightly longer swing. The wrists hinge and the hands come back to a spot about waist high. The backswing is a little steeper than it might be for shots from the fairway, because all your weight is on your left side. This steeper

Cindy Reid's Ultimate Guide to Golf for Women

angle should help the ball pop out of the sand as the force of the down-ward blow forces sand and ball up and out. Then you accelerate the club down and through the sand, making contact with your designated imaginary line and finishing the swing with your hips facing the target. As always, the follow-through is the same length as the backswing.

This down-and-through motion is particularly important when you have a buried lie. The leading edge of the club digs into the sand, and the force of this downward blow throws the sand into the air, and hopefully, the ball flies out with it.

■ *Practice makes perfect.* Okay, it's the oldest of clichés, but that's because it's true! The one surefire way to overcome your fears and phobias about the sand is to take a dozen or so balls into the practice bunker and work on getting them out. I'm amazed by the number of players who never bother hitting a single sand shot in practice, who then become frustrated by their inability to get up-and-down out of the sand. In no other area are expectations so high when preparation is so low. Sand play is like every other aspect of the game. If you don't practice, you probably won't be very good. But if you spend a little time working on your bunker play, you might just decide that playing in the sand isn't that bad after all.

Scoring Made Simple

Want to drop ten shots from your score? Want to cut your handicap in half? It's simple to do if you're disciplined enough to devote time to practicing the scoring shots. Mastering these will improve your scores and instantly make you a better player.

I KNOW IT'S A DIRECT CONTRADICTION to all the technical analysis you've seen and heard throughout your golfing life, but the golf swing is, at its root, a simple motion. You don't have to be a physicist to understand the principles of the swing, and you don't have to contort your body in ways only a prepubescent gymnast can appreciate in order to swing the golf club. You swing the club back with the shoulders, arms, and hands, and return it to the ball using your hips and legs to generate maximum speed at the nanosecond when club meets ball, an instant golfers call "impact." There's no magic or mystery. The motion is fluid and simple.

It's just not easy. And the difference between simple and easy rests in what our minds and bodies are accustomed to doing.

8 The Full Swing

I call the golf swing simple because it's not a complicated athletic move. You don't have to have good genes, great strength, perfect feel, God-given quickness, or agility to swing a golf club. With a little work, anybody can do it. I also say it's not easy, because the golf swing is one of the most unnatural moves you'll ever make.

Golf seems to defy every element of logic and common sense. For example, the only contact you have with the club is through your hands, but in order to hit a good golf shot, you have to relax your hands. Have you ever tried relaxing your hands to hit something? It's not easy. Nor is it easy to swing down and through a shot, hitting down on the ball and taking a divot out of the turf when your objective is to get the ball up in the air. Hit down to make the ball fly up? It doesn't make sense!

There are lots of other examples of the golf swing defying conventional wisdom. If you want the ball to curve right, you swing the club to the left of the target. And if you want the ball to curve left, you swing the club to the right. It seems backward, unnatural, and at times downright crazy, but that doesn't mean it's difficult. Granted, the golf swing can cause serious headaches if you don't understand how it works, but once you grasp the fundamentals of the swing, you'll find that the learning process isn't that difficult.

What Makes the Ball Fly Straight and High?

Everything you do in preparation to hit a golf ball—the grip, the setup, the backswing, the downswing, and the follow-through—is geared toward one millisecond, that moment when the club meets the ball. It's the only instant that counts. You can have the most rhythmic, classical golf swing in the world, but if you flinch at the moment of impact it means nothing. The ball will fly sideways (if it flies at all) and you will be left scratching your head and wondering what went wrong.

A good golf swing will produce maximum clubhead speed at the moment of impact. That means the clubhead has built all its momentum and is traveling at its fastest point at the exact moment it connects with the ball. Fortunately, we don't have to worry too much about accelerating the club at that point because gravity and physics take care of most of it. If you've ever seen or read about old-time sling shots—the kind where kids put a rock in a pouch connected by two strings so that swinging the pouch in a circle caused the rock to fly out—then you understand the physics of the golf swing. Your body swings the club in a circular motion, and if you follow a few swing fundamentals, gravity and momentum cause the club to be traveling at its fastest point right at the bottom of your swing where the ball is located.

MIT physicists and a few overbloated golf instructors call this "exterior circular motion creating linear force," which is techno-gobbledygook for "a good golf swing makes the ball go straight." But clubhead speed isn't the only thing that's important in hitting good golf shots. In fact, for women, it's well down the priority list. For women to hit consistently good golf shots the priorities are:

■   *Solid contact.* When Nick Price was trying to break into the profes-sional ranks, he asked his instructor what he needed to do to become a great player. The teacher took Nick's club out of his hands and pointed to the center of the clubface. "Hit the ball right in the middle of the face more times than anyone else, and you will become the best golfer in the world."

Nick did just that, becoming the number-one golfer in the world in the early 1990s. To this day he's one of the best ball-strikers in the game, because he still hits most of his shots in the middle of the clubface.

If I could wave a magic wand and make all the women golfers in the world do nothing else but hit the ball solidly in the middle of the clubface with every swing, I would be hailed as a miracle worker. Unfortunately, there's no potion I can give you or spell I can cast that will make you hit the ball every time in that area of the club we call the "sweet spot."

▶
Make a small move to learn the feel of solid contact.

In order to find that sweet spot and gain a sense of feel for making contact in the center of the club, I have my students start out making small moves, not even swings, but little motions where the clubhead never gets higher than the student's knees on either the backswing or the follow-through. This isn't a punch shot or a pitch or any other shot you would want to add to your repertoire. It is simply a drill that focuses on club meeting ball. The ball will only travel a few feet, but that's okay. As long as you get the feel for making solid contact, with the ball hitting that buttery smooth sweet spot in the center of the clubface, the drill will train your body to find that sweet spot as you progress to the full swing.

■ *Clubface square at impact.* This is one of the most confusing aspects of golf for women, not because we don't understand the concept, but the terminology often throws us for a loop. When you hear

someone (probably a man) say, "You have to square the club at impact," he isn't talking about a geometry problem or any other mathematical calculation. Squaring the clubface isn't like cubing a steak; it has nothing to do with a four-sided figure; and it has no relation to what children of the sixties called their parents (or what our children call us today).

A square clubface simply refers to a clubface that is pointing toward the target at impact. Square in this context means "neutral," not open or closed, but pointing directly down the target line.

This concept is critically important. You can't hit the ball straight unless the clubface is square at impact. In other words, the ball is going to go where the clubface is pointing at the moment of impact. If your clubface is open at impact the ball is going to fly to the right. If your clubface is closed, the ball will fly left. The only way for the ball to fly toward your target is for you to have the clubface square at impact.

The good news is, if you've gripped the club correctly, and if you've set up correctly before your swing, you shouldn't have to worry about the position of the clubface at impact. A square clubface at address should be returned to square at impact, all other things being equal.

But all other things aren't equal. Even though the club wants to come through square if we've set up correctly, golfers can't help but screw things up by trying to do too much with the club during the swing.

It's just natural, I guess. You're trying to hit a ball, and every synapse in your brain is screaming for you to tense up and thrash at it, beating it like a dirty rug. So you tighten your grip, draw back, and flail at it with all your might only to see the ball squirt to the left or right. If you had only relaxed, taken a deep breath, and ignored that little voice in your head screaming, "Kill it! Kill it!" you might have delivered the clubface squarely on line.

- *Swing path straight down the line.* The best way to describe "swing path" is through an example. Imagine holding one end of a rope with a heavy object suspended from the other end. Now imagine swinging the object back and forth, building momentum and speed with little rhythmic movements of your rope that create big sweeping movements on the other end.

But then something happens. Suddenly, you change the direction of your arm motion; you loop the rope going back and add another loop coming through. Now instead of having a smooth, fast path on which the heavy object on the end of the rope is passing, the rope is going in all sorts of different directions and the object on the end of the rope jumps around in spastic fits until it comes to a slow and gangly stop.

Now imagine your golf club as the rope in that example and your clubhead as the object being swung back and forth. With little effort your club passes along the same path back and through, moving straight back away from the ball and passing straight through toward the target. This causes the ball to fly straight and true. But if you interject any added and unnecessary motion into your swing—like tightening your grip at the top of the backswing and throwing the club at the ball or trying to scoop or lift the ball by flicking your wrists and lunging at it with your upper body—you disrupt that natural swing path.

The most common errors among women occur when tension creeps in at the top of the backswing. This causes you to throw the club at the ball with your arms and hands. Just like such a motion changes the path of your imaginary rope, this kind of lunging action moves the club onto a path that starts outside of your target line. At the moment of impact, the clubhead is moving on a path that is left of the intended target line, which means the ball might fly left of the target (a pull) or curve to the right of the target (a slice). The best shot an outside-in swing path produces is one that slices to a spot somewhere near the target. A solid, straight shot isn't an option.

Sometimes, women become so conscious of trying to lift or scoop the ball that they manipulate the club with their hands and wrists and change the path so that the clubhead approaches from inside the target line. At impact, the clubhead is moving on a path that travels right of the target line, which means the ball might fly right of the target (a push) or curve left of the target (a hook). A small minority of women have this problem, but I've had students who exaggerated this inside-out motion so badly they finished their swings looking between their arms.

A "square" swing path is one where the club is traveling straight down the target line at impact. If you can deliver the club along this path with a "square" clubface, your only option is to hit a straight shot.

Keep Moving
to Cut Down on Tension

If you haven't picked up on it from some of my earlier rants, let me shoot you straight: Tension kills. Tense muscles slow down your clubhead right at the moment you want to be generating maximum speed. Tension causes you to manipulate the club in ways that create odd and unnatural angles in your swing, and it forces the clubface into funky positions at impact. Not to mention the fact that it causes your hands and arms to hurt after a few hours of playing. I would estimate that of the thousand or so mishaps that are possible in the golf swing, ninety-nine percent of them are attributable to too much tension, either in the hands, arms, or body.

There are lots of ways to minimize tension—some, like acupuncture, are more radical than others—but one universally accepted method among golfers is to keep moving. The moment you freeze, your muscles tense up. If you keep moving, you build rhythm into your game and you stay loose. One way of keeping that motion going is to start every swing with a waggle.

The waggle, which is golf-speak for a fidget, gets your body into the rhythm of the swing, and provides a trigger mechanism for starting the swing. There are dozens of ways to waggle. Most involve moving your feet and shifting your hands and arms in such a way that you simulate the start of the swing. Sergio Garcia regrips the club like he's milking a cow, and Karrie Webb takes the club almost all the way to the top of her backswing as part of her waggle. Tiger Woods and Se Ri Pak have similar waggles, each hinging the wrists while patting their feet, and Annika Sorenstam and Laura Davies mimic the start of the backswings during their waggles.

Each of these waggles looks a little different, but the purpose is the same. Players waggle to melt away tension while preparing their bodies for the timing and rhythm of the swing.

You've probably seen people who don't waggle before their swings. They grip the club, set up, then stand over the ball like statues growing more tense by the second. Have you ever seen any of those people hit a good golf shot after standing over the ball for more than three or four seconds? I haven't.

Routine Waggles

While there is no universally accepted waggle, I teach my students to build their swings around a consistent preshot routine that starts from behind the ball. After picking a target line, gripping the club, and setting up to hit the shot, you should develop a routine that includes two or three waggles. Those waggles should simulate the start of your takeaway, with your shoulders pushing the arms, hands, and club away from the ball and returning the club back behind the ball along the path of your swing.

▶
This waggle simulates
the start of the swing.

Golf is about consistency and repetition. In order to build consistency into your game you need to develop your own preshot routine that puts you in a comfort zone, builds rhythm, and prepares you to swing the golf club. And you should never waver from that routine. Every shot should start with the same system—the same alignment, the same grip, and the same number of waggles.

I waggle the club twice before every swing, and I give a little speech to myself while moving the club back and forth behind the ball. "Fingers secure," I say to myself. "Relax your arms and shoulders; check your target one more time; now smooth it back and swing it through."

My preshot routine—including my waggle and the little speech I say under my breath—is like the beginning movements of a dance. Every aspect of the routine prepares me for the swing ahead. It's worked for me, and it works for hundreds of professionals around the world. There's no reason a similar preshot routine won't work for you.

The Moment of Truth

It's time to swing the golf club.

I've always believed that the first few inches of the golf swing dictate whether or not the shot you're trying to hit will be a success. During these first critical inches, your hands, arms, and shoulders set the club on its path or plane. Your weight shift, timing, center of gravity, shoulder turn, and extension are all determined in the first nanosecond of the swing, before your hands reach waist high and before the club is halfway back.

This is where managing tension through your grip, setup, and preshot routine pays off. Your hands should remain passive in the beginning of the swing, as the club is started back with the left shoulder and left arm working in sync to push it away. The clubhead stays low to the ground for the first three or four inches. There's no break in the wrists and no separation between your arms, shoulders, and chest. If you drew an imaginary line from the end of your grip, it should hit you somewhere between your sternum and your left breast. A few inches after initiating the swing with your left shoulder, that relationship should still be intact. The imaginary line from your grip should point to the same spot on your chest.

Golf pros call this a "one piece" takeaway, which means the shoulders, arms, and hands work together. Teachers like David Leadbetter say that the swing is "connected" if all the moving parts work this way, but I've never found a student who understood what that meant. The best analogy I've heard throughout the years came from Harvey Penick, who used to tell his students to imagine they were swinging a bucket full of water, and they needed to do so without spilling a drop. Harvey, a diminutive guy who used to teach wearing a sweater and tie, would actually demonstrate this technique by swinging a bucket of water back and forth. After years of practice he could make a pretty full swing without dumping water on himself.

There are plenty of other analogies teachers have used over the years. One of my favorites was the one where the teacher asked her students to imagine throwing a medicine ball two-handed down the target line. I always wondered how many of those students knew what a medicine ball was. I suspect that none of them ever threw a medicine ball to anybody.

Whatever mental image you need to draw for yourself is fine, as long as you let the left shoulder and left arm and left hand lead the club back.

The Killer Inside Move

The clubhead needs to travel along the target line as long as possible during the takeaway. That requires you to extend the club outward as you take it back. Too often players become so consumed by the thought of getting the club on an "inside" swing path that they move the club behind their bodies too quickly. This is called "laying the club off" on the backswing and it's a common flaw, even among the best players.

Tiger Woods struggled with laying the club off on the backswing before his 1998 swing change. Vijay Singh still struggles with it. It's his Achilles' heel, one I had to warn him about at the 2002 U.S. Open when I saw him on the range. "Don't lay it off, Vij," was all he needed to hear. Even major champions need a subtle reminder every so often.

If you move the club inside the line too quickly, you're forced to make compensating moves at some point in the downswing, usually at the top. If you don't, the club will get "stuck" behind you as you attempt to deliver it back to the ball, and the result will be a shot pushed badly to the right.

Cindy Reid's Ultimate Guide to Golf for Women

Creating the Magic L

As the hands continue to push the club away from the ball, your wrists should hinge to bring the club up off the ground. This is where women have trouble. Our hands and wrists aren't as strong as those of men, so a lot of women tend to either pick the club straight up, flexing their elbows and lifting the club with their bodies rather than hinging their wrists, or they roll their wrists, forcing the club behind their bodies and creating the false illusion that their wrists are doing the work.

The proper wrist hinge sets the club in a position where the butt end of the grip (that section of the club that was pointing at your chest at setup) is now pointing at the ground, and the shaft of the club and your left arm form the letter L.

This is the most important position in the entire golf swing! If you can set and maintain your L throughout the backswing and well into the downswing, you will hit the ball long and straight. Sure, there are other things you need to do in the swing—like move your hips through the shot and shift your weight properly from your right to your left side—but none of these motions is as important as setting your L and keeping it in place as long as possible.

To illustrate this to my students, I sometimes hit balls while kneeling on the ground. These shots don't go as far or as straight as the ones I hit while standing, but they go a lot farther and straighter than many of the best shots my students hit. I don't do this to demoralize anybody. I do it to illustrate how important the arm–club L is to the golf swing. It is the hinge that creates clubhead speed and allows you to deliver the club squarely back to the ball at impact.

◄

The shaft and left arm form an L, a magic position in golf.

The Pivot

Once your L is set, the rest of the backswing is simple. All you have to do is rotate your shoulders, twisting your torso so that your left shoulder turns under your chin and the club is raised to a point above your right shoulder. The majority of your weight is on your right side during this turn, and your left foot comes up off the ground a little bit.

A lot of instructors will tell their female students to keep their hips still while turning their shoulders. This is called the "coil" approach to the golf swing, and it is the most universally accepted method for building power into the swing. I find that most women golfers don't have the flexibility or strength to keep their hips still throughout the backswing. When they try to keep the lower body still, they compensate by lifting the club with their hands and arms instead of turning their shoulders, or they cut their backswings off before the club gets shoulder high.

I don't want my students making pirouettes on the first tee, but I also don't want them restricting their golf swings because of some vague notion about keeping their lower bodies rigid. The shoulders should turn more than the hips. For the flexible and athletic among us, the ratio between the shoulder turn and hip turn can be substantial. But for most golfers, the left foot needs to come up off the ground a little and the hips should turn along with the shoulders in order to get the club in the proper spot on the backswing.

At the top of the swing, the shaft of the club is parallel to the ground, and if you drew an arrow out from the clubhead, it would point straight toward your target. If the club drops below parallel, you've probably loosened your grip or hinged your wrists in a way that distorts your L. The same is true of a club that points somewhere other than down the target line. If the club points left of the target at the top of the swing, you've "laid the club off," which means you've flapped your wrists rather than hinging them properly. If the club points right of the target (or "across the line" in golf-speak) you've lifted the club with your hands rather than letting your shoulders and wrists do all the work.

The proper backswing has the club set directly over the right shoulder with the left arm fully extended and the shoulders turned as fully and completely as possible. The club points right at the target, and the L, while having moved all the way to the top of the swing, still remains intact. From here you're ready to generate clubhead speed with precision and accuracy at impact.

The keys to getting the club into the correct position on the back-swing are:

- Start the backswing with your left shoulder turning under your chin and pushing your left arm, hand, and the club away from the ball.

- Keep the club moving along the target line as long as possible. Don't let it fly inside too quickly.

- Turn your shoulders around a relatively stable right leg, but let your left heel come off the ground a little so that the majority of your weight is on your right foot at the top of the backswing.

- Your right arm comes away from your body on the backswing, but at the top of the swing, the elbow is pointing toward the ground.

- The shaft of the club is pointing down the target line at the top of the backswing.

- Your head remains still and your spine angle remains unchanged throughout the backswing.

◄

Club "laid off"
(pointing left of target);
club "across the line"
(pointing right of target);
club "square" at the top
(pointing at the target).

Unwinding Toward Impact

The top of the backswing is like the "set" position a sprinter gets into before the starting gun goes off. Your body is coiled; your left arm is extended; your hands are in the perfect position; your weight is on your right side, behind the ball so that you can spring forward like a leopard; and your hips are poised for action. Before I ever played golf I was a pitcher for the U.S. Fast Pitch Softball team, and I like to think of the top of the backswing as being like the windup for a 100 miles-per-hour fastball. The only thing left to do is unwind your body and let it go.

That's easier said than done. The problem with the downswing is that our brains are screaming "Hit it! Hit it! Hit it as hard as you can!" So we do what our brains tell us. We throw the club at the ball from the top of the backswing, and lunge forward and down, tightening our legs to brace for impact. Usually this results in a shot that rolls down the fairway a few yards or one that shoots off at a screwy angle to a spot somewhere other than the fairway.

This is natural. The club is in your hands, so you think that you have to use your hands to hit the ball. This causes you to break your L angle early and move the club out of the path (or plane) you've worked so hard to establish. You lose clubhead speed, because you've broken your L angle, and the likelihood of you delivering the clubface squarely onto the ball is slim at best.

In all good golf swings, the lower body initiates the downswing. This is where women should have a great advantage over men if we just use what Mother Nature gave us. Women have hips. Our bodies are designed for us to do a lot of work between our navels and our knees in life. Women golfers who learn to use their lower bodies in the golf swing hit the ball great distances with tremendous accuracy even though they lack the upper body strength of many men.

My friend Michelle McGann is a good example. Michelle isn't massively strong. She can't bench press twice her body weight or rip off five sets of fifty-pound curls. She's a woman of average upper body strength. But Michelle hits 290-yard drives with great regularity. How does she do it? She uses her lower body to initiate the swing and generate clubhead speed.

By rotating your left hip, bringing your left heel back onto the ground and turning your lower body toward your target, the shoulders, arm, and club are pulled down into the perfect preimpact position. Your L remains intact, and your weight shifts from your right side to your left side, putting all the power of your body weight into the shot.

There are many different ways of feeling this sensation. Ben Hogan and Nancy Lopez said they felt the downswing was initiated by turning (or "clearing" or "firing") the left hip toward the target. Jack Nicklaus and Judy Rankin said they felt the first move was firmly planting the left foot on the ground, which initiated a shifting of their weight and got their lower bodies turning toward the target. Greg Norman and Laura Davies feel like they are pushing off with their right feet, again initiating the lower body turn and weight shift.

All these sensations have one thing in common: They all focus below the navel. None of the great players feel as though they start the downswing with their hands and arms. They all create power in their swings by using the biggest, strongest muscles of the body: those between your belly and your knees.

▲

See how my hips move at the beginning of the downswing?

I initiate my downswing by feeling as if I'm turning my left hip toward the target. This starts my weight shifting from my right side to my left side and pulls my shoulders and arms into what we golfers like to refer to as "the slot," that perfect preimpact spot where maximum clubhead speed is only moments away. I feel as though I'm still holding my L angle, waiting for the perfect moment to let the wrists go and swing through the ball and toward the target.

The sequence goes like this:

- The lower body unwinds and you shift your weight from your right side to your left side.

- The shoulders, arms, and club are pulled into a preimpact position by this uncoiling process.

- You maintain your L as long as possible.

- The club enters the perfect, preimpact slot.

To Impact and Beyond

Now comes the easy part. If you have done everything right up to this point, the clubhead will be traveling about seventy to ninety miles per hour and there's little you can do to manipulate or control it. The wrists unhinge and the clubhead is delivered onto the ball at the exact moment the club is traveling its fastest. Your weight is on your left side, and your hips and shoulders are still turning.

Because the club is traveling so fast, I try to get my students to think about things other than impact; things like where the club should be after impact; or where their shoulders, chest, and hips should be during the follow-through. To try to have someone think about the split second when club contacts ball is pure folly and usually does more harm than good. What you should note, however, is how similar the impact positions are of all good players.

Man or woman, big or small, good players might have different-looking golf swings, with differing speeds and differing approaches, but at impact all good players deliver the club to the ball in almost exactly the same way. You should sear these images into your brain and remember them as you try to create your own perfect golf swing.

I focus on a spot directly in front of the ball and on my target line. If I'm hitting an iron, I try to hit down on the ball and drive the head of the club into the ground at that spot in front of the ball, and if I'm hitting a wood, I try to sweep the

▼

Everything in the swing is geared toward this; the moment of impact.

clubhead along the grass at that spot as well. If I'm swinging well, my iron shots will hit the ball first with a descending blow, then hit the ground knocking out a divot.

This descending blow imparts backspin on the ball and causes it to fly into the air. Wood shots don't require as much spin, so they are struck with a more sweeping motion than are irons. But never, ever should you swing "up" at a golf ball. This is one of the most common and most serious errors I see among women. They think that in order to get the ball up in the air you have to swing up or "scoop" the ball. The only problem is, that sort of swing imparts topspin on the ball, and the resulting shot rolls on the ground.

This usually prompts one or more of your playing partners to say, "You looked up," or "You didn't keep your head down on that one." I've seen women reduced to tears over such comments. They know that if they looked down any longer or harder they might get cricks in their necks, but they still can't stop topping the ball. That's because they don't understand the mechanics of getting the ball airborne. Hitting down on the ball gets it into the air. Scooping the ball causes it to roll on the ground.

When I first learned the game, I became obsessed with this concept. Like most players I hit more than my fair share of topped shots or "thin" shots that screamed off the club about waist high with little or no spin. I vowed never to hit such shots again, and spent hours on the range hitting down on iron shots until I dug trenches in the ground in front of the ball. Unfortunately I took things to the extreme. After one long session I felt a pain in my left side. A couple of days later I went to the doctor and discovered that I'd cracked two ribs from hitting the ground so violently. I don't recommend you take it that seriously, but

you need to spend some quality time focusing on the path of the club immediately after impact.

▲

Everything is moving down the target line on the follow-through.

From there, I teach my students to stand straight up, face the target, and enjoy the results of a perfectly struck golf shot. If you've done everything correctly, your weight should be on your left foot, your hips and chest should be facing your target, and the club should flow nicely into a finish position somewhere over your left shoulder. If you find that you are catching your balance or stumbling forward or rocking back onto your right foot or that your feet have moved to a different spot on the ground, you haven't made a solid, balanced golf swing, no matter what the results of the shot. I tell all my students that they should be able to pick up their right foot and remain perfectly posed on their follow-through. If they can't do it, they need to work on their balance.

The impact and follow-through sequence goes like this:

- Head still and spine angle still intact, the club releases when the right arm is straightened, the L finally broken, and the clubhead hits the ball.

- You have to think "down and through." Hitting down on the ball creates backspin and causes the ball to fly high and long. Most good women players don't do this enough. They need to hit down on a lot more shots, focusing on hitting the ball first and the ground second.

- Finish in balance. Swing slowly for a while if you have to, but do whatever it takes to make your swing a perfectly balanced dance.

Putting It All Together

Unfortunately, the golf swing isn't about still positions or static angles. The operative word is "swing," a fluid motion perfectly choreographed to produce a long, straight, solidly struck golf shot. In order to build your own swing, you have to understand how all the parts fit together. The golf swing is like a ballet. When executed properly it is graceful and fluid, seemingly effortless in its simplicity and artistic in its form. Watching players like Annika Sorenstam, David

Duval, Michelle McGann, and Vijay Singh hit balls is like watching a
Twyla Tharp dance production or listening to a Yo Yo Ma concerto.

You, too, have a personal artistry and an inner rhythm that will
carry over into your golf swing. If you walk fast, talk fast, eat fast, and
have difficulty sitting still, chances are good that your golf swing will
be quick. If you are deliberate in everything you do, never seeming to
get in a hurry no matter what the occasion, you will likely carry that
slow personal rhythm into your golf swing.

I've also gotten pretty good at defining people's personalities by watching their golf swings. Dottie Pepper, for example, has an aggressive, often combative personality, and she has an aggressive, attacking golf swing. Karrie Webb is quiet and consistent in her personality, and her golf swing is fluid and consistent with no wasted motion or effort. Tiger Woods has a fierce and often fiery personality, and that's the way he swings the golf club, while David Duval is a methodical, slightly bashful plodder. Those traits are also evident in David's swing.

You can't be something you're not in golf. If you're a little hyper-active in life, you can't slow your natural rhythm when you're on the golf course, and if you're a slow walking, slow talking go-along-and-get-along kind of woman, you won't suddenly become the Terminator once you put a golf club in your hands. What you can and should do is work within the framework of your body and your biorhythms to craft a golf swing that's right for you.

Building Balance
and Finding Your Swing

- -

As much as I would love to say that if you sleep with this book under your pillow you will wake up with the perfect golf swing, the game is a lot harder than that. Building a swing takes time, patience, and a lot of practice. But there are some drills you can work on to shorten your learning curve and speed up the process of building a solid golf swing.

■ *Swing with your feet together.* A good golf swing is a balanced golf swing, and one of the best drills I've found for building balance is to hit balls with your feet together. If you make the common mistakes that come naturally to most golfers—throwing the club from the top, lifting and lunging at the ball, picking the club up with your hands and slapping at the ball to scoop it into the air—while your feet are together you will either swing and miss or lose your balance and fall down or both.

This drill also helps you develop your own sense of timing and swing speed. Arnold Palmer, who has always had a quick swing, doesn't

- -

▲ This is a great drill for building balance.

slow his swing down when he's practicing this drill at home in Latrobe, Pennsylvania, and Ernie Els, who has a slow, silky swing, doesn't speed his swing up when he's working on the range, either. Everybody has a natural swing speed. You'll find yours quicker if you spend time hitting balls with your feet together.

■ *Fold your arms and swing without a club.* The movements of the upper and lower body in golf are so radically unnatural that I always make my students spend time in front of a mirror turning their shoulders and rotating their hips with their arms folded across their chests. This gives you the feeling of the swing without the mess and fuss of actually swinging a golf club.

The big muscles of the shoulders, torso, hips, and legs must move with subtle synchronicity in order for your swing to repeat time and time again. The best way to develop these dance steps is to practice without a club until you feel comfortable turning your shoulders and rotating your hips back and through the swing.

▼

Develop the feel of the swing by practicing with your arms folded.

■ *Hit a tee, not a ball.* Too many players become obsessed with whacking the ball. Teachers call that being "ball bound," so tied up in knots by the thought of hitting the ball that you can't relax and make a good, solid golf swing. One of the best ways to overcome that ball-bound obsession is to eliminate the ball from the picture. Try hitting a tee instead of the ball. You aren't likely to tense up when swinging at a tee because you know it doesn't matter how hard you hit it. The tee is only going to fly

▲

Plastic balls allow you
to focus on your
swing, not the results
of the shot.

about five or six feet even if you make a perfect golf swing. You should
still set up to the tee just as if it were a golf ball, but because it's not
a ball, you can focus on making a good, fluid swing and not on your
results.

■   *Hit plastic balls at home.* If you want to advance one step
beyond hitting a tee, but still work on your swing without worrying
about the ball, go to your local discount sporting goods store and buy a
pack of plastic balls. These usually come six or eight to a pack and
they cost about fifty-cents a ball. If you hit them well, they might
travel twenty or thirty yards, but they will give you the feeling of setting up to swing through a golf ball without the psychological hurdle of
worrying about the shot. You can focus on the swing, not the result.

■   *Hit balls into a net.* The best drill, and the one that has shown
the most positive and dramatic results, is to hit balls into a net. Of
course, this requires you to buy a net, but if you want to improve at a
rate fifty to seventy-five percent faster than average, it's an investment
you'll want to make.

Hitting balls into a net accomplishes two goals: It gives you the feel of hitting a real golf ball, but it eliminates any anxiety you might have over where the shots are going. You can focus on the fundamentals of your swing without worrying about the results. Documented results show more rapid improvement from players who practice hitting balls into a net than from players who work exclusively on the driving range.

- *Swing a weighted club.* This requires another purchase, but it's also worth every penny. Swinging a weighted club conditions your muscles to swing the club along the correct path, and it keeps you from making the common mistakes of picking up the club with the hands or throwing the club and breaking the L at the top of the backswing. Weighted clubs are simply too heavy for you to make those errors. And if you do, you will feel it immediately.

You also can't overswing a weighted club. It's too heavy to swing quickly. So if tempo and timing are your primary concerns, this is the drill for you.

▼
I swing a weighted club at least 25 times a day.

Changing a Championship Swing

Tiger Woods arrived on the professional scene with the biggest splash the game had ever seen. He won twice in his first seven starts as a pro, and eight months after turning pro and four months after his twenty-second birthday he showed up at Augusta National for the Masters as the odds-on favorite to win his first major championship. Not only did Tiger exceed expectations, he shattered the Masters scoring record, shooting 18-under-par for seventy-two holes and winning the tournament by an astonishing twelve shots.

A week later, Tiger sat down with his instructor, Butch Harmon, and viewed the tape of the tournament. But Tiger didn't like what he saw. "I almost threw up," he said of the swing he saw on tape. "I had a perfect timing week. I knew that swing wouldn't hold up forever."

So Tiger did the most remarkable thing imaginable: He took a swing that had just demolished the field at the Masters and he changed it. "I was getting the club way across the line at the top," he said. "I knew I needed to tighten up my swing if I wanted to win a lot of tournaments for a lot of years."

Butch and Tiger worked for eighteen months on revamping the championship swing. During that period Tiger only won once on the PGA Tour and once in Asia. But he knew he was close. Finally, hitting balls one day on the back of the range at his home club in Orlando, Tiger picked up his cell phone and called Butch. "I've got it," he said. Butch didn't need to ask what his star student meant. Tiger had finally grooved the changes in his swing and gotten comfortable with the more compact, solid swing technique.

From that point forward Tiger put together the most remarkable stretch of championship golf in the history of the game. He won ten worldwide events in 1999, and another ten events in 2000, including three of the four majors. When he won the Masters a second time in 2001, Tiger became the first man in history to hold four professional major titles at the same time.

Would it have happened if Tiger hadn't embarked on the ambitious swing changes he and Butch agreed to early in the 1997 season? "No way," Tiger said. "I knew I needed to change some things, and I did it."

Indeed he did.

Finding That Extra Ten Yards

Every female student I teach wants the same thing. "I want to hit the ball farther with my driver," I hear countless times.

I usually respond to this by throwing it back at the student. "Okay," I say. "What do you think you need to do to gain that extra yardage?"

The answers range from "Hit it harder with my hands," to "Take it back farther," to my personal favorite, "Close my eyes and pray a lot."

None of those answers is correct (although a little prayer never hurt anybody). There are, however, a few things you can do to build more distance into your swing.

■ *Swing full but try to hit it short.* The first drill I give to students wanting to increase their distance is to hit balls with the driver swinging as full as you can—a complete takeaway and full follow-through releasing the club at impact—but try to hit the ball as low as possible and only carry it about 100 yards.

This drill improves your balance, your timing, and your ability to hit the ball squarely in the middle of the clubface, all critical elements to hitting it long.

A lot of people are shocked when I tell them that to hit it long you have to work on hitting it short, but that's the case. Distance comes from precision timing, solid contact, and perfect balance. This drill will help you develop all three.

- *Extend your backswing as far as possible.* The longer you can extend the club along the target line on the backswing, the farther you will hit the ball. If you lift the club or take a shallow, narrow backswing you might make great solid contact, but the ball won't go very far. To add distance to your game, you need to create arc, and arc comes by extending your backswing as far as possible.

Laura Baugh learned that lesson a little late in life, but it still worked wonders for her. Laura was one of the shortest but straightest drivers on the LPGA Tour for the first fifteen years of her career. Then she realized that short and straight wasn't going to cut it in the modern game. For the next two seasons, she worked on increasing her distance by extending the club as far away from her head as possible on the backswing. "I moved my hands back as far as I could keeping the club on plane the entire time," she said.

As a result of those changes Laura went from one of the shortest hitters on tour to one of the longest, averaging over 275 yards in driving distance at age forty-four.

You can do it too. As you're hitting balls ask yourself, "Can I extend my hands any farther away from my head on the backswing? Can I get the club any farther away from the ball and still remain on plane? You probably can, and if you do, you'll definitely hit it farther.

- *Get stronger.* Golf isn't a game of brute force, but you can't deny the fact that stronger players do hit the ball farther. Later in these pages, I devote a chapter to physical fitness and the importance it plays in your golf game. If you're serious about improving your driving distance, you should take that chapter to heart. A stronger, fitter, more flexible you will hit the ball farther and better.

Puring the Irons

have a student who is on the brink of moving up from an adequate, intermediate player to being a good player. She drives the ball beautifully and is plenty long. She is one of the most naturally gifted putters I've ever coached. Her feel on the greens is extraordinary. The only thing holding this player back is her inability to hit her approaches anywhere near the putting surface.

This is true for a lot of players. They hit their drives in play, and they have no trouble putting when they get to the green. It's those in-between shots that create all the problems.

I've found two consistent problems with players who struggle with their irons:

1. They consistently underclub, not hitting a long enough club for the shot required.

2. They do not hit down crisply on their iron shots.

The first of these is easily remedied. When I realize that one of my students has trouble with her irons, I ask her, "How far do you hit a 5-iron?" If the answer comes back "About 150 yards," which it usually does, I take her out onto the golf course and pick a spot I know to be exactly 150 yards to the hole. "Okay," I say, "let's hit 5-irons." When she comes up short time after time, I discreetly go to the bag and come back with a 4-iron or a 3-iron and say, "Let's give this one a try." It only takes a few shots with the correct club for a player to realize the error of her ways.

The second flaw is a little tougher to fix. Most women, including some of the best players in the world, don't hit down crisply enough on their irons. The ones who do make good crisp contact with those clubs are the ones you see winning week after week on the LPGA Tour. The others struggle with distance control and consistency because they never hit the ball in the clubface the same way twice.

Here are some drills I recommend to help you hit down on more iron shots:

- *Hit balls from a downhill lie.* Take a 7-iron or a 5-iron to a spot on the range where you can set up with your left foot well below your right, a substantial downhill lie. The best spot is usually right in front of the tee where the ground slopes down toward the range.

From this spot, you should hit at least a bag of balls a day working on hitting down and through each shot. For a while, you won't be able to hit down on it at all. You'll miss a couple, hit a few fat, then thin a few head-high screamers down the range. But once you get the feel for hitting down on those shots, you'll be stunned by how good these shots feel. In addition to helping you pinch down on your irons, this drill helps you set the club on plane on your backswing, and it forces you to move your weight through the shot on the downswing. It's one of the most complete and effective drills I prescribe for my students who are looking to make the jump to the next level.

- *Cut off your follow-through.* Taking a full swing with your irons, focus on hitting down and through, but then cut off your follow-through as quickly as possible. I don't want you to stick the club in the ground. Just cut off the follow-through as quickly as you can. If you do this properly, you'll never stop the club before it reaches waist high on the follow-through. But that's not the point of the exercise. What you'll discover is that by cutting off the follow-through, you're also working

the club down the line more effectively, and you'll hit down and through more iron shots.

- *Turn the stripe of the range ball upward and try to hit it.* The method I used when I cracked my ribs (not that this drill produced the injury) was to turn the stripe of the range balls upward to about the two-o'clock position, then try to hit down on the stripe. This took a lot of time and discipline, but it eventually worked for me. If you've got the dedication, it will work for you as well.

Fairway Woods

Women carry more fairway woods than men. Sometimes women take it to extremes, carrying things like 9-woods, 11-woods, and even 16-woods, clubs I couldn't imagine hitting but that some women swear by. No matter what configuration of woods versus irons you carry, you should know the fundamentals of hitting a fairway wood. The sequence for nailing your fairway woods goes like this:

- *Position the ball forward in your stance.* These clubs more closely resemble your driver than your irons. Position the ball in your stance accordingly.

- *Take an in-between stance.* Your stance isn't as wide as it might be if you were hitting a driver, but it's certainly wider than the one you would take for a middle- to short-iron shot. Shoulder-width is a good rule of thumb.

■ *Relax your hands.* Because woods require more of a sweeping swing than a down-and-through action, you must start your swing with relaxed hands and a turn of the shoulders. Tension in the grip kills any chance of hitting good solid fairway woods.

■ *Sweep the club back long and straight.* Just as you would if you were hitting a driver, you should sweep the club back along the target line as long and as far as possible.

■ *Keep your head still.* As much as any shot in golf, the fairway wood shot requires you to keep your head still and your spin angle intact. There isn't a lot of margin for error with fairway woods. To hit them crisply you have to keep your head still.

■ *Swing through to the target.* A lot of players screw up their fairway woods shots by slapping at the ball just before impact. The best way to avoid that trap is to visualize a smooth finish, with the club swinging outward toward the target. If you keep that smooth follow-through in your mind, you have a very good chance of hitting a great shot.

Great Players Learn to Work the Ball

Have you ever seen a great player who was faced with a difficult shot, a carry over water into a rugged headwind or an approach shot to a tucked pin where a tree limb was intruding on the line? If so, were you amazed at how the player shaped the shot to fit the situation? You shouldn't have been. All great players learn to work the golf ball. It's what separates the good golfers from the great ones.

Fairway woods are an important part of the women's game.

If you're ready to make the jump from good to great player, you need to practice shaping shots, hitting balls low, high, left, right, hard, easy, and straight. This isn't easy. Only the most accomplished players should try it. But it's essential if you're looking to take your game to the next level.

Some of the shots you need to learn include:

■   *The knockdown shot*. This is a low driving shot that stays under the wind and rolls once it hits the ground. In order to hit this shot, you have to play the ball back in your stance (somewhere in the middle for a long iron or fairway wood), keep your lower body passive, and trap the ball against the turf with your hands leading through impact.

In the beginning you'll hit a lot of these shots fat. Don't worry. If you work on pinching the ball down with your hands leading the club through impact, you'll eventually start hitting low screamers that are great for windy conditions.

■   *The power fade*. Shaping a shot from left to right on command is tough, especially if you've spent most of your golfing life trying to overcome a slice. But the power fade is a shot you have to add to your repertoire if you want to become a great player. In order to learn it, you should practice lining your feet, hips, and shoulders left of the target, opening the clubface so that it faces the target, then taking the club outside the target line on the backswing, and swinging to the left of the target. You want to keep the club from turning over at impact when you make this swing, so feel like you are hanging on to the club throughout the follow-through. This is the one shot where you don't want the club to fully release.

The ball will curve severely at first. But the more you practice this shot, the more comfortable you will become at controlling the amount of fade you put on the ball.

■ *The draw.* You also need to learn to curve the ball to the left. You accomplish this by playing the ball back in your stance, lining up right, closing the clubface, and swinging from an inside path. The danger with this shot is letting your hands get too active. You want the club to release, but the tendency is to pick up the club with your hands and slap at the ball at impact. This causes you to hit the shot off-center, and it could go anywhere.

To hit a controlled draw, you have to relax your hands and initiate the swing with your shoulders, just as you would if you were trying to hit the ball straight. The closed clubface and inside-out path will affect the flight of the ball. Your hands should be as passive as possible throughout.

In the beginning you'll hit a few duck hooks, shots that never get more than head high and hook so quickly you could hang dresses on them. But with practice, you'll learn to control the spin of the ball and the curvature of this shot.

Patience Pays

The biggest asset to developing a good full golf swing is patience. The game cannot be mastered in a day, a week, a month, or even a year. Steady improvement and persistent dedication to the fundamentals of the swing are the hallmarks of success in our game. If you want to be in this game for the long haul, you need to stick with it.

GOLF WOULD BE A LOT EASIER, and a lot more boring, if golf courses were as flat as plywood. Think about it: You'd never have to worry about an odd bounce or a shot over this hump or that knoll; topped or thin shots would roll forever; and all putts would be dead straight. You'd also never have any odd lies where the ball is above or below your feet or where you have to stand uphill or downhill to hit a particular shot. Yes, the game would be a lot easier. But I can't imagine anything duller.

Part of the challenge of golf is the complexity of the terrain on which the game is played. Tennis, cricket, and other outdoor sports

9 Odd Lies (Or "Up the Down Fairway")

don't offer this unique perspective. If you travel to France to play tennis, you're going to play on the same shape and size tennis court you could find at any park in New Jersey. But every golf course is different, with different length holes, different topography, and differing demands on your game. The links courses of England and Scotland are windswept and treeless, and the rolling topography offers some maddening bounces. Many Florida courses are flat and full of forced carries over sand, trees, and marshland. Wyoming offers some of the most spectacular elevation changes I've ever seen on a golf course, while the rolling hills of the Northeast are home to some of golf's great masterpieces.

In order to enjoy the intricacies of the game, it's important that you learn how to hit shots from all sorts of unusual lies. Some of these lies will be found in the rough or off the beaten path, but you'll find a few of them right in the middle of the fairway. No matter where you encounter them, it's best to be prepared with an arsenal of shots for every conceivable lie.

Uphill Lies

With all uneven lies, you have to pay particularly close attention to your setup. When your left foot is higher than your right and you're trying to hit the ball from an uphill lie, the natural tendency is to let all your weight hang back on your right side. Gravity is pulling you in that direction anyway, so why not let nature take its course, right? Unfortunately, if you stay on your right side, the only two shots possible are a fat flub or a screaming duck hook, one of those head-high heart-in-your-throat shots that is bound for the bushes from the moment it leaves the clubhead.

This is easily avoidable. First, you should play the ball slightly forward in your stance, about an inch left of center. Then you need to evenly distribute your weight while insuring that your shoulders are in line with the hillside. This is going to feel like all your weight is on your left side, since gravity and momentum are pulling you to the right. Don't worry. Setting up with your weight on your left side is the least of your worries from this kind of lie.

No matter how strong or talented you are, chances are good that you're not going to get your lower body turning through the shot with the power you generate when swinging from a level lie. Because of this, the club will most likely be delivered from the inside, and hook or draw spin will be imparted on the ball. That means your shot is going left, and there isn't much you can do about it. Rather than stand there befuddled by the fact that your shot is traveling left of target, I tell my students to line up right. You know the ball's going left. Play for it.

▼

Note the ball position from an uphill lie.

You're also going to have a tendency to hit the ball higher and shorter than normal off an uphill lie. In addition to not getting your normal amount of power behind the shot, your club is traveling on the same path as the hillside, which means the ball will up-shoot off that incline. To minimize the potential problems this fact of physics creates, take one or two more clubs, choke down slightly on the grip, and take a slightly less than full swing. A solid three-quarter 5-iron from an uphill lie will get the job done a lot more often than will a fully swung 7-iron from the same spot.

Downhill Lies

The most dreaded lie in the game is the one where the ball is perched on a downhill lie and you are addressing it with your right foot higher than your left. What makes this shot so treacherous is the shot it's likely to produce. Because gravity is pulling you forward toward your target, the tendency is to slide your upper body down the hill during the swing. This puts the club on an odd angle at the moment of impact and the ball catches that area of the club between the hosel and the clubface. The result is a shank, a word a lot of golfers won't even utter. It's a low, squirrelly abominable shot that feels even worse than it looks. The shank is the most reviled shot in golf, which makes the downhill lie shot, with its propensity for causing shanks, one of the most frightening in the game.

It doesn't have to be that way. For starters, you should play the ball toward your high foot, about an inch or so right of center, and align your shoulders with the hillside. Once again gravity will try to pull you down the hill, so you should fight that tendency by evenly distributing your weight.

▼

My shoulders remain parallel to the ground, even on a downhill lie.

Of course you can't fight gravity forever. During your swing you are likely to make a pronounced move down the hill and to your left, which means the club will likely impact the ball with an outside-in path. This means the shot is going to curve right. It's also going to come off the club lower than your normal trajectory. The hill and the path through impact delofts whatever club you're swinging.

Rather than stew about a low, driving shot that ends up curving right of target, play for the shot you know is coming. Aim left, make as smooth a swing as possible while keeping your balance, and play for the fact that the shot is going to come out lower than normal.

Ball Above Your Feet

Sometimes golf balls seem to defy gravity. There's a slope in the fairway that your ball catches, but rather than rolling to the bottom of the slope, the ball stays on the hillside leaving you with a lie that looks more like something out of T-ball than golf. The ball is perched above your feet, knee high or higher at times, and you're wondering if you should trade in your golf clubs for a Louisville Slugger aluminum bat.

Don't fret. This shot is easier than it looks. First, you have to understand that when the ball is above your feet, your swing plane is naturally going to be a little flatter. You're standing more erect and swinging around your body more than normal to make contact. You can offset this to some degree by taking one more club than you would normally need and choking up a couple of inches on the grip. This will help, but it won't solve your dilemma. You're still going to swing flatter than you would if the ball were on level ground.

Your clubface is also pointing left. The higher the ball is above your feet, the farther left the clubface is pointing at address. This means if your swing is perfect, the ball is going to fly to the left. Rather than invent a new swing to compensate for this fact, simply line up to the right and try to swing the clubhead right of your target. The ball will jump off the club on the path the clubhead is traveling (right of target), but it will curve back on line because of the angle of the clubface at impact.

It will take some time and practice to gauge how far your shots will draw and how far right of target you need to align your body in order to hit the shot you want, but that practice will pay off in almost every round of golf you play.

▲

With the ball above my feet I aim slightly to the right.

Ball Below Your Feet

- -

Those same balls that defy gravity by clinging to hillsides above your feet also stubbornly stick to hillsides where you have to stand above them and lean forward just to ground your club.

- -

▲

With the ball below my feet I focus on staying down and through the shot.

When the ball comes to rest on a hillside below your feet the first thing you have to do is modify your setup. The natural tendency, and the one you have to avoid like cheap hair color, is to slump your shoulders in order to reach the ball. This kills any chance you have to hit a good shot. You must make a conscious effort to keep your back straight by sticking your bottom out even farther than you do in your normal setup, bowing a little more at the waist, and adding a little more flex to your knees. In the most severe cases of the ball being below your feet, you might have to widen your stance and bend your knees like a downhill skier. But those shots are rare, and when they do arise, it's best to take your wedge and chip the ball back onto a lie you can manage. For the standard industrial ball-below-your-feet lie, the most important thing is to set your body in a position where you can swing the club without lifting, shifting, sliding, or lunging at the ball.

Once your posture is established, you should know that your swing plane is going to be steeper than normal, and because of the angle of the hill, the clubface is pointing right of the target when your body is perfectly aligned. This is just one of those facts of nature and physics that you can't fight. The only way to make this fact work to your advantage is to accommodate for it by lining up left and swinging the clubhead left of the intended target. Your shot will start left, but the angle of the clubface will cause it to curve back on line.

This, too, will take some practice. But you can't imagine the thrill you feel when you pull this shot off during a round.

Playing from a Divot

How many times have you hit a perfect shot only to find your ball nestled into an unrepaired divot left by some insensitive boob who played ahead of you? In casual rounds with friends this is usually not a problem. Someone will likely say, "That's not right. Roll it out of that hole," and you're all too happy to oblige. But there will come a time, be it a tournament round or a friendly competition that gets a little less friendly as the match heats up, where you will have to play a shot from a divot. Knowing what to do in this situation could save you a stroke or two, and could mean the difference between winning your match and going home to gripe about the bad break you caught.

▼

A nasty lie, but one you need to learn to play from.

In order to turn a bad lie in a divot into a good shot, you have to adjust your setup so that the ball is more toward your right foot, an inch or two back of center. This will allow you to hit down on the ball with a steep descending blow. You also need to close the clubface slightly to compensate for the new ball position.

Once you've made these setup adjustments, you simply take your normal swing with an added emphasis on driving the club down

▶

When the ball is sitting
down, play it back in
your stance.

and through the shot so that you nip the ball cleanly. You will hit the
ball lower than normal, so plan your shot accordingly. But with a little
practice, you will also impress your friends by turning a bad break into
a miraculous recovery.

Ball Abutting the Fringe

A lot of good shots roll into bad or unusual lies, but none is more
frustrating than the shot that lands on the green and rolls to the
edge of the putting surface only to butt up against the fringe.
Your ball is on the green, but there's this wall of high grass behind it.
You can't take your normal stroke with the putter, because you can't
take a backswing without hitting the fringe. You've seen Tiger Woods
putt with his 3-wood in situations like this, but you've never tried or

practiced that shot, and to do it while playing doesn't seem smart. So what do you do?

The answer is simple: You chip it. Even though your ball is on the green, there's no rule requiring that you use a putter. If the grounds crew has maintained the course in such a way that a chip shot is required from the green, you shouldn't hesitate to hit the shot they have given you.

With a lofted club, a wedge or sand wedge, and playing the ball well back in your stance, make a small, left-arm-and-shoulder-led stroke, hitting down on the ball and popping it on line and toward the hole.

In the 1930s and 1940s, back when several of the game's biggest tournaments were match play rather than medal play events, the rules called for something known as stymies. If a player found her ball was blocked by another ball on the putting green, she was stymied. The only way to negotiate a stymie was to chip the ball over the ball that was in your line of play, even if it meant using a wedge (or mashie in those days) on the putting surface.

Byron Nelson was a master at this shot, chipping shots in the hole from stymied positions so often that some people thought he was better with his wedge on the greens than he was with a putter. Byron and the other players of that age didn't worry about hitting the "accepted" shot in those situations. They played the shot the conditions warranted, no matter what club it required.

You should do the same.

▼

Don't hesitate to chip from the green if that's the only shot you have.

Recovery Shots:
Do No Harm

Everybody who has ever played golf has hit the ball into trouble at one point or another. The more you play, the more times you are likely to visit the rough or the trees. The best players in the world, the ones who play golf every day, find trouble a lot more often than the amateur who only plays once a month, simply because good players put in more rounds and have more opportunity to make mistakes than the women sitting at home.

But even though the best players in the world make mistakes, they rarely compound those mistakes by trying something silly from the rough. The first rule of trouble shots is to get the ball out of trouble. If you've hit it in the trees, don't compound that mistake by making another mistake trying to hit a miraculous recovery. Get the ball back in play, back on the fairway or somewhere near the green, where you can minimize the damage to your score.

A student of mine has a hard time with that concept. I watch her walk into the rough or the trees with a 3-wood in her hands and I say to myself, "What is she thinking?" Invariably, she leaves the shot in trouble or creates even greater problems for herself. When I say to her, "Why would you play that shot under those circumstances?" she replies, "I needed to go for it."

Going for it is one thing. Costing yourself a chance at par by attempting something foolish is quite another.

I can't blame all these bad habits on students. When I was making my debut appearance at the LPGA qualifying school only two years after I first took up the game, I only needed to shoot even par on the final day to earn my tour card. That seemed simple enough. I'd broken par every round up until that point. Another under-par round would move me well up the list of qualifiers.

Then on the first hole, I hit my drive into a fairway bunker. "Just take a short iron out and get it back in play," my caddie said. "You can make par from the fairway."

I was having none of it. The first hole was a par-five and I was going to make birdie. More than that, I was going to show the rest of these future LPGA players how great I was at pulling off miraculous shots. I drew out my 3-wood and crawled into the bunker. I waggled a couple of times, picked a perfect line, and hit the ball solidly and purely into the lip of the trap. It ricocheted back and plugged in the bunker. Before the carnage was complete I'd made a 10 on the first hole. It was a lesson I never forgot, and one I've tried to ingrain in all my students.

When you hit a shot in trouble, you should consider the conditions, analyze your options, and hit the shot that will cause the least amount of damage while getting you back into play. Never try a shot you haven't practiced and never, ever, leave a shot in the rough or in the trees. The purpose of hitting a recovery shot is to recover. If that means taking a 7-iron and making a one-quarter swing to punch out of the trees and back to the fairway even though you're 200 yards from the green, then that's what you do. To pull out a 3-wood and rip it at the flag in the hopes that the ball will fly between two trees and under the limbs of a third is foolishness in the extreme. The chances of pulling that shot off are minuscule, and the penalty for failure is high. From the fairway you have a chance to make par. From deeper in the trees you're looking at double bogey or higher.

▶

The first rule of
trouble shots is:
Get out of trouble.

The same is true with a ball that's nestled down in the rough. Even if you're only 150 yards from the green, if you don't have the lie to hit the shot you know, take out a wedge and get the ball back in play. Compounding your mistake by leaving the ball in the high grass will only frustrate you and unnecessarily elevate your scores.

Trouble-shot Rules

I have a checklist I give to all my students to help them execute trouble shots. It's a common sense preshot routine, one you would be well served to jot down on a card and carry with you for a while until the routine becomes a habit.

The list reads:

* **Visualize the shot you want to hit.** Think about it and play it out in your mind. Is it doable? Have you ever done it before? Is it the smartest shot for the situation?

* **Check your lie.** How well is the ball sitting on the ground and how will that affect the type of shot you wanted to hit?

* **Choose your club.** This is the moment of truth. Select the club you know is right for the shot you need to hit.

* **Take a practice swing.** Build positive images in your mind and in your muscles for the shot you are about to hit.

* **Pick your target.** If you need to fly the ball to the edge of the green, pick a spot—a leaf or a discolored blade of grass—and visualize the ball flying to that spot.

* **Set up.** Position and align your body for the shot you have decided to play.

* **Execute the shot.**

It's that simple. If you follow this checklist, you'll be stunned how many strokes you shave off your score.

IF YOU'VE SPENT ANY TIME around the game, you've probably heard someone utter the most worn adage in golf. It usually follows a shot of some luck where a player bounces a drive off a tree, tops an approach shot into the bunker, then hits a high-flying sand shot that lands in the hole for birdie. After jumping about in adulation, this golfer digs into the cliché bag and says, "Hey, it's not how; it's how many."

After all these years, such fortune-cookie profundity should result in a two-stroke penalty or an automatic loss of hole, especially when the person uttering such blather has no idea what the phrase means. The old "It's not how; it's how many" nugget originated as a tamer replacement for the graphically gross "There's more than one way to skin a cat" chestnut, that many of us cat lovers found offensive.

10 Playing the Game

Both these Confucius-style lessons tell us that golf is as much about strategy as it is about power and athletic prowess. At the end of the day, you aren't judged in golf by how far you hit the ball or how pretty and classic your swing is. Our game has a very objective measurement for success. The player who shoots the lowest score wins. Golf scorecards don't have brackets or lines for style points, and there are no figure skating-type judges sitting behind every green rating you on your poise or artistic interpretation. If you make a three on a hole and your opponent makes a four, you win. How you did it is irrelevant.

This is a simple concept, but even the most advanced players easily forget it. How often have you heard a tour player sum up his or her round by saying something like, "I hit the ball really good today, but I didn't get much out of my round," or "I'm really pleased by the way I hit the ball"? These sound bites make good television, but they're meaningless when it comes to the biggest question, which is, "What did you shoot?"

I run into this quite a bit. Because my club is also the home club of the PGA Tour, I play a fair amount of golf with various pros from the men's tour. Although I'm reasonably long off the tee for a woman, I don't come close to hitting the ball as far as guys such as Vijay Singh, David Duval, or even Gabriel Hjertstedt. But that doesn't mean I can't compete with these guys. They might hit driver, 3-iron to the par fives while I'm hitting driver, 3-wood, 9-iron the same distance, but if I make four on the hole and they make four on the hole, we've tied the hole. It doesn't matter how we did it. If I hit a 4-iron approach to the middle of the green on a par four while someone who has outdriven me by fifty yards hits 9-iron at the flag, but misses the green, who's in better shape? I have a twenty-foot putt for birdie, and my playing partner is faced with a delicate and difficult little chip.

Know Your Game
and Play Your Game

t's awfully tempting when I'm playing with the guys to try to keep up; to try to gauge my driving distance against the men and try to outdo them by sticking my iron shots closer to the holes. Not a round goes by that I don't have a chat with myself on this subject. Emotionally I want to go after them. I want to take a wide stance on the first tee and rip my tee shot as hard as I can. I want to hear the greatest players in the world say things like, "Good shot, Cindy," and I want to see the looks on their faces on the fairway when my ball is a little closer to the green than theirs. But intellectually I know this is the kind of folly that leads to embarrassment. That's not my game. I'm not as long, strong, or powerful as the men who play golf on tour for a living. To be sucked into playing their game instead of my own would be a tragic error, one that would lead to high scores and great frustration.

If Vijay hits the ball 320 yards, and I hit the ball 255 yards, he has a distinct advantage (as he should since he's consistently ranked among the top-ten players in the world). But if I try to keep up with Vijay's drives by swinging harder or hitting shots that are outside my normal repertoire, not only will I fail to catch him, I probably won't hit the fairway, which means I will have compounded my mistake.

In order to be competitive with the boys, I have to hit the ball in the fairway, and be smart when I'm hitting my approach shots into the greens. I can't hit a high, towering 3-iron with lots of spin. My shot patterns are lower and softer. So when I'm faced with a 3-iron approach shot, I forget about where the pin is located and hit the ball into the center of the green. In most cases, I never have more than a twenty- to twenty-five-foot birdie putt when I execute this shot properly.

If I try to hit my 3-iron at a closely tucked flag with rough or a bunker nearby, the chances of the ball ending up in a bad place go up. Sure, I might hit a great shot that ends up a few inches from the hole. I might even hole it for eagle! But I have a much greater chance of missing the green and making bogey. The payoff could be great, but the

▶

Why fire at the flag, when playing to the middle of the green is both smarter and safer?

risk is huge. On the other hand, if I hit the shot I know into the center of the green, I also might make birdie by holing a twenty-footer. The worst I should make is a par. And it would take a terrible set of circumstances for me to take three putts and make a bogey.

By playing my own game instead of someone else's I keep birdie as an option, insure that I'm going to make par, and all but eliminate bogey from the equation. This is smart golf, the kind of disciplined, strategic thinking that separates winners from losers, good players from marginal also-rans.

Impossible Shots Are Just That—Impossible

I can't count the number of times I've seen amateurs try to hit shots they couldn't execute if they practiced golf every day for the rest of their lives. I've seen a woman whose best tee shot travels 200 yards in the air try to hit a 220-yard shot over water to a well-guarded green, then stare in disgust when the ball lands in the water. I've had a student who couldn't hook the ball if her life depended on it, try to hook a 3-wood around a dogleg. She failed and hit a perfectly straight shot that soared thirty yards into the woods. And I've seen women who never hit the ball higher than their heads take dead aim at towering flora thinking that somehow they might magically hit the highest shots of their lives over the impediment. Of course they never do, and they huff and puff when the shots end up in the brush.

It's amazing how golfers let their imaginations run away with them. They see Tiger Woods hit a shot on television, so when faced with a similar shot, they say to themselves, "I can do this." But they can't, and deep down they know it.

I find that women are guiltier of this than men. Perhaps it's our natural sense of optimism or our innate creativity, but the women I teach are far more apt to try an impossible shot than are their male counterparts. That's not to say men don't do boneheaded things on the golf course. They can pull some real head-scratchers. But women surprise me at times. Intelligent, logical, rational, conservative, professional women who never go to the market without a reasonable plan of action make some of the most irrational decisions I've ever seen on the golf course. They try shots that aren't just outside the scope of their capabilities; they attempt shots that are impossible. The best women golfers in the world wouldn't try to hit a 200-yard shot over water to narrow green from a questionable lie in the rough, but I have students who never think twice about going after such a shot. When the ball plunks in the water, these women seem distressed, even angry! "Why are you upset?" I always ask. "That shot was bound for the water the second you took the club out of the bag."

This glib retort doesn't sit well with some. I should probably be a little more sympathetic given the loss of a ball and the added penalty shots my students have to add to their scores in this situation, but it's frustrating to watch women make such silly mistakes. Before you hit any shot in a round, you need to ask yourself a few questions:

- *How many times have I hit this shot in the past?* If the answer is "none," you need to forget that the shot ever entered your mind. Even if you have hit the shot you are imagining once or twice in your life, that's probably not enough times for you to try to pull it off. Ben Hogan never hit a shot in a round that he hadn't hit at least 100 times in practice. Karrie Webb says she tries to perfect every shot in practice before attempting it in a round, and Tiger Woods works for months on one shot just in case he might need it at a critical moment in a major championship. You should learn from the experts. Don't attempt a shot you don't know.

- *How does the shot in question jibe with the way I'm hitting the ball today?* If you're having one of those days where you couldn't hit water if you fell out of a boat, trying a shot that hits double-digits on the difficulty scale isn't the brightest of decisions. Before you attempt any shot, measure its chances of success against how you've hit the ball during the rest of the round. If you've sliced the ball all day, you probably aren't going to pull out a beautiful, high draw from a tight lie behind a tree. You should always gauge a shot's potential by how well or how poorly you are swinging that day.

- *What do I gain from trying this shot, and how does that compare with the consequences for missing it?* I'm stunned by some of the high-risk shots I see my students try just to get the ball a few yards closer to the green. I actually had a student who once tried to punch a shot through the fork in a tree when simply pitching out sideways would have left her in virtually the same position. To the surprise of no one except the woman attempting the shot, the ball hit the tree and ricocheted deeper into the woods. She took a quadruple bogey and never recovered. If she had hit the shot perfectly, the best she could have hoped for was a lay-up that would have left her thirty to forty yards short of the green. If she had pitched out sideways—a straightforward shot with no hazards or impediments—she would have been left with seventy to eighty yards to the flag. Was the prospect of being forty

◀

Examine all your
options, then hit the
shot with the highest
likelihood of success.

yards closer to the green worth the risk? I can't imagine how anyone could have thought it would be, but this woman tried it anyway.

You shouldn't fall into the same trap.

Know Your Distances

The other big mistake my female students consistently make is misjudging how far they can hit the ball. This works both ways. I've had students who consistently hit their 3-woods 190 to 200 yards who, when faced with a 130-yard shot, pull out the 3-wood as if it's the perfect club for that distance. Then I've had students who, once in their lives, hooded the clubface of a 7-iron from a flier lie with a twenty miles-per-hour tailwind and hit the ball 150 yards. Since that time they've always pulled the 7-iron whenever faced with a 150-yard shot.

Neither of these situations makes a lot of sense. The woman who hits the 3-wood from 130 yards always flies the ball too far, causing herself unnecessary grief and hardship. The woman who insists on hitting the 7-iron from 150 yards is deluding herself, and costing herself plenty of lost shots. Both these women should probably hit 7-irons from 130 yards, because, on average, that's how far they hit their 7-irons. But because they've never taken the time to calculate the average distance they hit each of their clubs, they are clueless about what club to pull from any given distance.

The distance you hit a club isn't the distance the ball travels with the wind behind you or when it's sitting on a tuft of grass in the rough. You should know how far you hit each club in your bag in windless conditions and average temperatures from decent but not perfect lies.

If you only hit your 7-iron 140 yards when you cream it, and you hit it 125 yards when you miss it, but the average distance you hit the 7-iron is 130 yards, then you hit your 7-iron 130 yards. You should gauge all your shots on the course accordingly.

That doesn't mean you should draw the 7-iron like a saber every time you're faced with a 130-yard shot. If you have a healthy wind in your face, the shot will play a good bit longer than 130 yards. You might need a 6-iron or even a 5-iron in that situation. If the wind is behind you, you might need an 8-iron or 9-iron. If the lie is a little iffy, you might want to take a slightly longer club and make a shorter, smoother swing to insure solid contact. And if you're between clubs—you are at a distance that is a little too long for a 7-iron but a bit too short for a 6-iron—you should choose the longer club and concentrate on making a smooth swing.

All these situations require you to know how far you hit each club in your bag. As you're practicing, pay attention to your distances. Ask your pro about the distances to certain landmarks on the range, like flags or trees, and see how close you are coming to those landmarks. On the course, don't hesitate to step off a distance that might have deceived you. If you hit a solid 6-iron in windless conditions that falls thirty yards short of the green, have your playing partner drive the cart forward while you step off the distance of your shot. You might be surprised by what you find.

You should also keep a diary of each round you play where you write down the number of greens you missed and how and where you missed them. If you find at the end of a round that you've missed ninety percent of your greens short, you should reexamine the clubs you're hitting. You aren't going to hit the ball as far in cold weather as you are in warm, balmy conditions, and you don't hit it as far at sea level as you do in Lake Tahoe where the air is thin. But until you examine and evaluate your misses, you'll never know whether or not you're hitting the wrong club from certain distances. Keep track of these stats. It will pay huge dividends on your scorecard.

Keep a Log and Review Your Rounds

Speaking of a shot diary, the best evaluation tool you have for improving your scores is a full-fledged shot diary, a small notebook or pad where you write down every shot in a round, how you hit it, where it ended up, and what the conditions were. If you read this diary after the round, you'll probably be surprised by what you find.

For example, I saw one of my students in the lounge after she had begun keeping a regular shot diary. "How did you play?" I asked.

"Gosh, Cindy, I hit the ball great, but I just didn't score well."

"Well, let's have a look at the shot diary," I said. After a couple of minutes of reading, I said, "What do you mean by 'hitting the ball great.' It looks like you only hit one green in regulation, and the majority of your misses were long and left."

"That's the thing," she said. "I was catching the ball so pure, but it was flying longer than I've ever hit it in my life and going left."

I explained to my student that this is a common phenomenon. Because of either a flaw in her setup or a slight flaw in her swing this student was pulling all of her iron shots. This caused her to hood or close the clubface, turning a 7-iron into a club that more closely resembled a 5-iron. "These shots have a sneaky way of feeling great when they're coming off the club," I told her. "But you can't control the distance, and you're going to miss everything to the left."

She nodded and looked through her diary again. "You know," she said. "I missed most of the fairways to the left today, too. I never would have thought about it if I hadn't written it down."

Most people wouldn't. That's why keeping records and reviewing them after the round is so important. Once you analyze where and how you are missing most of your shots, you know what parts of your game need the most work. You can also chart your progress and keep records of your improvement. It's a great tool for goal setting and a great way to keep yourself focused.

GOLF IS ONE OF THE FEW GAMES you can enjoy playing by yourself. Tennis wouldn't be a bundle of laughs if you didn't have an opponent. My college basketball team wouldn't have won many games without a full complement of players. Even board games like Monopoly and Clue aren't much fun alone. But golf is different. You can go out solo and have a blast. When David Duval was first learning the game, he would tee off at sunrise, and he wouldn't stop until the sun was so low on the horizon he couldn't see his ball. Rarely did David have a playing partner. Someone else in the group would have slowed him down, and he

11 Competition and Fun

didn't need to play with or against anybody. The golf course was enough of a challenge.

Golf and downhill skiing are the only two athletic activities I've undertaken where you don't need anyone around in order to be challenged. In skiing it's just you against the mountain, with the clock as the ultimate arbiter. You will never master the sport. You can only improve your time and learn to respect the mountain. Golf pits you against the course with Old Man Par standing watch as the final scorekeeper. Like downhill skiing, you will never master golf, never bring the course to its knees, and never reach perfection. You don't need an opponent, a partner, a referee, or a teammate for golf to be a challenge.

The course is your opponent and your friend. It gives; it takes; it lures; and it shuns. It is the ultimate competitor and the perfect companion.

You've probably heard pros on television say they "don't play the other players," they "play the golf course." For many, that seems like an odd concept. If you're in a tournament, of course you're playing against the other players. If you aren't, why are you there? But those who compete know what these pros mean. The goal in playing competitive golf is not to beat everyone in the field; it's to shoot the lowest score you possibly can. The end result of that low score is a win. You beat the rest of the field by beating the golf course.

Some of my biggest challenges in golf have come when no one else was around. Early in my golf career I stood on the seventeenth tee needing two pars to break 70 for the first time. This was a huge goal and a great accomplishment if I could pull it off. The fact that no one was around to see it was irrelevant. I was playing the golf course, competing against my own personal best score. With or without another player nearby, the pressure to par those last two holes was palpable.

You may or may not have experienced this sensation in your golfing life, but if you stick with the game long enough, you will. Annika Sorenstam, as successful as she has been on the LPGA Tour, still searches for something she calls "54 vision." According to Annika: "You can, conceivably, birdie every hole in a round, thus shooting 54. Nobody's ever done it, but it can be done. Someday it probably will be done. I'd like to be the one to do it." No mention of beating her arch rivals Karrie Webb and Se Ri Pak in that declaration. Other players are incidental to the goal. If Annika or anyone else shoots 54, she will beat everyone else and set a record for the ages. By beating the golf course, she will, as an added bonus, beat all her fellow competitors.

Ben Hogan was a master at this. One legendary story has one of the pros in Hogan's group making a hole-in-one on a par three. After great applause and much celebration, Hogan and the other members of the group finished the hole and walked to the next tee, whereupon Hogan turned to the man who had just had the ace and asked, "What did you have on the last hole?" Whether or not the story is true is irrelevant. No one who ever knew Hogan would argue the point: He focused so intently on beating the golf course that he was oblivious to what other players around him were doing. There were times when Hogan's wife, Valerie, would walk eighteen holes with her husband, and she would later ask, "Did you see me at all today?" He was the model of focus: a steely competitor who knew that winning meant beating the golf course, not the other players in the field.

You probably don't and won't take the game quite as seriously as Ben Hogan and Annika Sorenstam, but that doesn't mean you shouldn't set goals for yourself and measure your successes against a personal benchmark that has nothing to do with other players.

If you have trouble imagining yourself playing alone, here are some games to make solitary golf a little more interesting:

- **Two-ball match.** If you're out on the course alone, one of the most intriguing games is a two-ball match. In this game, you play two balls off each tee and keep score with each. At the end of eighteen holes, you total up your scores and see which ball wins. I do this a lot. I'll mark each ball differently with a black Sharpie—one black dot on ball number one and two black dots on ball number two—and I'll play a match with myself with each ball. If ball one wins a hole, it has the honor on the next tee. The only thing my balls can't do is concede putts. I agree with myself on the first hole that all putts will be holed and all appropriate penalties added.

This is fun. You'll find yourself grinding over putts trying to keep the match as even as possible with both balls. It can even get a bit schizophrenic. I've found myself trash-talking my own golf balls. It's probably a good thing no one else was around.

- *High ball; low ball.* This is another great two-ball tournament. In this one you play two balls on each hole, but rather than separating the scores for each ball, you keep the lowest score and the highest score for each hole. If you make scores of five and six on the first hole, and five and seven on the second hole, your low-ball score shows two fives, and your high-ball score shows a six and a seven. This is a great game, because your low-ball score will usually be better than your average, and your high-ball score will be a little worse than your average. The challenge is to keep both scores as close as possible.

- *Scramble.* On those days when you need an ego boost, go out alone and play a two-ball scramble. In this game, you hit two balls from the tee, choose the best one, and play two shots from that spot. You continue picking the better of your two shots throughout the round. If you miss your first putt for par, don't fret. Just make it the second time. Your total in this game should be a good deal lower than your average score. It's a great way to boost your confidence and realize that you can, indeed, shoot lower scores.

- *The one-more-club game.* This one tests your shotmaking, your ability to craft shots and manufacture swings when needed. You tee off on the par-fours and par-fives with one ball, but, from that spot, you hit two balls into each green. The trick to the game is that the second ball is always hit with one more club than the first. If you hit a 7-iron into the green with ball number one, you have to drop a second ball in the same place and hit a 6-iron. If your 7-iron shot came up short, you're probably okay with a 6-iron. But if a 7-iron was the right club, you have to either hit a knockdown 6-iron or manufacture a swing that doesn't hit the ball over the green.

This is a great game to enhance your creativity and shotmaking skills. Before your round is through, you'll find you're much more aware of things like swing speed, contact, and shot trajectory, variables you might not otherwise have pondered. Your scores will also surprise you. Even if your second ball is a little long at times, you probably won't score any worse, and you might score better with the second ball. It's a lesson in club selection as much as it is a lesson in crafting and creating shots.

Games for Two or More Players

As fun as solo golf can be, you probably didn't take up the game for its isolationist qualities. Golf is as much a social outlet as it is a competitive sport. People take up the game to enjoy the company of their family, friends, and neighbors in a pristine outdoor environment. Some play golf to meet new people, others use it as a business tool to entertain clients, while others like to compete in friendly games with other like-minded enthusiasts. Whatever your reasons for playing golf, there are plenty of friendly games to meet your goals and needs.

Match play—the most common form of competition. On any given day at clubs around the world, the most common games are being contested under a form of play known as "match play." Match play is different than the events you see the pros play on television in that your total score in match play is irrelevant. You're playing another person in your group in a match. If you win a hole, you are one hole up, or 1-up, as match-play scorers would say. If you lose the next hole, the match returns to being tied, or "all square," and if you lose another hole, you fall one hole down, or 1-down.

What makes match play interesting is that each hole is like its own separate tournament. If you make bogey on the first hole and your opponent makes double bogey you still win the hole and go 1-up in the match. If you birdie the next hole and your opponent holes a shot from the fairway for an eagle, you lose the hole and the match falls back to all square.

You don't have to finish every hole in match play, because your score doesn't matter. If your opponent makes a four, and you still have a ten-foot putt for a five, pick it up. You've already lost the hole. You can also concede putts in this format. If you've made a four, and your opponent has a short putt for a four (to "halve" the hole in match play lingo), you can, if you choose, say to her, "Pick it up. That's good," and move on to the next tee. Some players use the concession strategy to their advantage by conceding short putts early in the match, but forcing their opponents to putt them in the later holes as the match tightens. This adds to the pressure of a close match, and it's a crafty way to get under your opponent's skin, if you're inclined to do such things.

A match is won or lost when you're either up or down by more holes than you have left to play. So if you're 3-up after the sixteenth hole, you've won, because you only have two holes left. In match play–speak, you're said to have won your match three and two, or 3-2.

These sorts of games are uncommon in the professional ranks, because it's almost impossible for 100 or more competitors to compete in matches in a week. The PGA Championships was the last major to abandon match play as a format after World War II, but the U.S. Amateur (both men's and women's), the British Amateur, the Senior U.S. Amateur, and Mid-Amateur Championship are still contested in match play, as are the Ryder Cup, Walker Cup, President's Cup, and Solheim Cup. Both the PGA Tour and LPGA Tour have reintroduced match play events to their schedules with some success. The format is an important part of golf's rich heritage. I'd hate to see it evaporate from the professional scene.

Week-in and week-out match play is, by far, the most popular format at the club level. It's a game you can enjoy with your friends and one where you can build healthy competitive rivalries.

■ *Best-ball matches—also called "fourball" matches.* There are all sorts of games you can play under the match play umbrella. The most popular is the two-woman best-ball match, which is sometimes called a "fourball" match. In this game, you and your partner play against two opponents with only the best score for each team counting. So if you have a three and your partner has a four, your score is the team score for that hole. If one of your opponents has a four and the other has a five, they count the four as their team score, and you are 1-up for the match.

This format is great when you have players of different skill levels. If two members of your group are pretty good players, and the other two are just learning the game, splitting up teams so that one good player and one beginner are partners on each team makes for a competitive, balanced match. It also cuts down on embarrassment for those who are new to the competitive scene. With a partner to carry the day, if you hit your ball in the woods or the water or you have difficulty extracting yourself from a dreadful sand trap, you can pick up. Your partner's score will count as the low-ball score for that hole.

If match play is the most common format at clubs throughout America, the best-ball or fourball match is the most popular match play game. It allows four women to choose teams and compete with and against each other in a fun, nonthreatening way. If you haven't tried this game, you should.

■ *Scramble.* Most women I teach love to play in a common club game known as a "scramble." This is a team competition with two, three, or sometimes four women on a team. Each player tees off, your team chooses the best shot, and everyone plays from that spot. You continue in this manner until the ball is holed, and you play all eighteen holes in this way.

Scrambles are the least intimidating, most fun events you can play. If you miss a tee shot, it's no big deal because you have teammates who can bail you out. If you're a decent putter, but you have trouble hitting drives, you can contribute to your team by making a few putts. If you drive the ball well, but you struggle with your irons, you can contribute by hitting tee shots to spots most of your partners have never seen. And if you love your wedge, but can't hit any of the other clubs in your bag, you can contribute by nestling a few short shots close to the hole. By the end of the round, everyone on a scramble team will have contributed and everyone will walk away feeling good about her round.

- *Alternate shot or "foursomes."* One of the most challenging two-woman team formats is alternate shot, or "foursomes." In this game, two players play one ball alternating shots until the ball is in the hole. You can modify this somewhat so that both players tee off, then choose the best shot and alternate from there, or you can assign one player as the driver for each hole. There are plenty of neat ways to massage this format so that it's fun for everyone.

  Unfortunately there's no way to eliminate the pressure you feel when standing over a shot. Not only is there no backup if you hit a poor shot, if you hit it poorly it's your partner who suffers. I've seen women reduced to tears in alternate shot competitions. It's fun, but it's tough. And there's nothing like an alternate shot tournament if you want to test a friendship.

- *Points, or Modified Stableford competition.* Another popular format is the points-system competition, often called a "Modified Stableford." In this game, points are assigned for various scores on each hole. A bogey usually accounts for one point, a par is worth two points, and a birdie is worth four points. If you're skilled and fortunate enough to make an eagle, it's worth eight points, and any score larger than a bogey doesn't earn any points. At the end of the round the player with the most points wins. This scoring system is designed to promote aggressive play. One birdie can offset a number of mistakes, so you are better served by being more aggressive than by playing conservatively.

  You can modify this format even further depending on the skill levels of the participants. If most of the competitors in your group have trouble making pars, then simply modify the format so that double bogey counts for one point, a bogey is worth two points, and a par is a four-pointer. Nothing is cast in stone. Be as creative as you need to be in coming up with your own game. The purpose here is fun and competition, with neither being more important than the other.

Answering Questions and Resolving Disputes

Rarely does a week go by that I'm not asked at least one rules question. These can range from where and how to take a drop for a ball that's in a hazard to what sort of penalty is incurred if you hit the ball into an unplayable lie. Even though I know the answers, I always make a point of digging a rules book out of my golf bag and looking up the answer for my students. "Wow, you have a rules book in your golf bag?" they say.

▼
Always carry a rules book.

"I've always had one in my bag, and you should too," I answer. "If a situation comes up on the golf course, it's best to have the rules book handy so there's no dispute."

This shocks a lot of my students. They've never played a game where the rules book is carried by a majority of competitors, and the lofty language the USGA uses to tell you how to spot a ball or take a drop intimidates them. But the more you know about *The Rules of Golf*, as published by the USGA and the Royal and

Ancient Golf Club of St. Andrews, the more prepared you will be when questions of procedure arise.

You can buy a rules book at most golf shops. You can also pick up plenty of supplementary material that will help you understand the intricacies of the rules.

The main thing to keep in mind, however, is that golf is supposed to be fun. If you break a few rules along the way, so be it. As long as you aren't playing in a competition, and as long as you know what the rules are, you can choose to play by them or not. It's completely up to you. But if you do want to be competitive at some point in your golf career, even if it's only at your local club, you need to know the rules and be prepared to play by them when the time comes.

Handicaps

During a recent lesson I asked one of my new students if she had an established handicap. "Well," she said, "my eyesight is not very good anymore." Being the model professional that I am, I lay down on the ground laughing. Then my student and I had our first educational session on golf's handicapping system and what it means to establish a handicap in golf.

The handicapping system, designed and run by the USGA, is a numerical rating meant to level the playing field for players of all skill levels. The lower your handicap, the better player you are. Professionals have handicaps on the negative side of zero (or "scratch," as a zero handicap is called). Most amateurs have handicaps ranging from one to thirty, with various fractions added just to confuse things.

I'm not going to venture into the mathematics of the handicap system since it involves things like third standard deviations and aggregate variances. What you should know, however, is that by posting your scores in the handicap computer at your club every time you play, the computer will eventually come up with an average based on your scores and the difficulty of the golf course you're playing. From there the math wizards take over, and you are issued a numeric handicap.

The reason this is important is because you might want to play in a match with or against someone much better or worse than you, and the handicap evens things out. If you have a handicap of twenty and you're playing with someone who has a handicap of twelve, that player needs to spot you eight shots. That means, on the eight most difficult holes on the course, you get a one-shot advantage over your fellow competitor. If you have a five on one of those holes, and your competitor has a four, you tie (or halve) the hole. If you have a four and your competitor has a four, you win because you have been given a shot on that particular hole.

In stroke play competitions, the handicap system evens out the scoring so that someone who has an average score of 100 can compete with someone who shoots in the 70s on a regular basis. The system is marvelously efficient as long as all players are honest in posting their scores. Once you've played a few times, look into establishing a handicap as soon as possible. You'll have a lot more fun when you can compete with everyone on an even field.

PART THREE:

Beyond the
Course

THERE ARE A LOT OF WAYS of looking at golf. You can view it as a Tuesday morning pastime, something to do between yoga and picking up the kids from school. You can look at it as a business tool, a forum for meeting new clients, entertaining old ones, cultivating relationships, and closing deals. Golf can be a family activity, a way of spending several hours with your spouse, significant other, children, parents, or siblings. Or, if you're like me, you can view golf as a lifestyle, a vehicle that broadens your social, physical, business, personal, and spiritual horizons. No matter how you choose to view golf, there are a number of off-course activities that will improve your game and make you feel better about yourself.

12 Fit for Golf

Because I came to golf late in life after spending my teens and early twenties competing in other sports, it never occurred to me to look at golf as anything other than another athletic endeavor with its own unique physical requirements. When I began asking questions about exercise physiology and physical training for the game, I was stunned by what I learned. The general response I got was, "What are you talking about?" followed by hearty laughter at my naïveté. I didn't get the joke at the time, but I soon realized that not only are most golfers totally ignorant of the fitness requirements and physical demands of the game, they laugh at the notion of working out to improve their golf scores.

Fortunately times have changed. In the last decade golfers have come to grips with the fact that strength, flexibility, and overall fitness play a critical role in the game. Stronger, fitter, more flexible athletes hit the ball farther and straighter, have better touch around the greens, and respond better under pressure in the closing holes than do their weaker counterparts. Golf is more than a game; it's a sport. And as is the case in all athletic sports, fitness is crucial.

Annika Sorenstam was a great player before she started working out, but it wasn't until she embarked on a full-fledged strength and fitness program that she became a record-setter. In two short years Annika increased her strength by fifty percent and doubled her flexibility through weight training, stretching exercises, and cardiovascular workouts. She reportedly does 1,000 crunches a day, which many of her competitors viewed as the impetus of her rising-star success. To keep up, players like Laura Diaz, Lori Kane, Vicki Goetz-Ackerman, and Marisa Baena pay regular visits to fitness performance specialists who tailor workouts for their specific needs.

Kane hits the weight room regularly, saying, "The buzz words [on the LPGA Tour] now are 'improving your core muscles.' I wouldn't have tried this a few years ago, but you look at somebody like Annika and she's a fine-tuned machine. She handled all the stress she faced out there, and I found by the end of the last season I was starting to fatigue by the thirteenth, fourteenth, and fifteenth hole."

Se Ri Pak also added fitness and strength training to her agenda, saying, "Everybody is so strong now. If we want to stay where we are, we have to work that much more."

The most popular spot, other than the range, on the PGA Tour these days is the fitness trailer, a rolling gymnasium and performance-enhancement center traveling with the tour each week. On any given afternoon, you can find Justin Leonard on the treadmill, David Duval doing crunches with a weighted ball on his chest, and Ernie Els lifting dumbbells and stretching. All these players (and over 100 on all tours) employ personal trainers who develop sport-specific workout programs to improve strength, flexibility, and stamina. Els, a longtime skeptic of the golf-fitness craze, now works with a personal trainer every week. "With stretching and toning and cautious training we have developed a program that fits my needs," Els says. "My swing now has more speed. My shot-making is a lot more consistent, and I have more power and flexibility. I feel looser and stronger. And, just as important, my fitness program has strengthened my mind. Working out can pick up your moods and really help turn a bad day into a good one."

Every professional is on the fitness bandwagon now. Even Jack Nicklaus, who warned for years about the dangers of weight lifting to the pliability of golf muscles, pumps iron with a trainer. Greg Norman, a longtime fitness buff, has even installed a portable minigym on his private jet so that he can get in a workout at 30,000 feet.

Don't kid yourself: 300-yard drives and overpowering iron shots aren't solely due to advancement in equipment technology. Today's golfers are stronger, fitter, more flexible athletes than their predecessors. This new emphasis on fitness shows in the increasingly lower scores on all tours.

Nobody expects one-round-a-week amateur golfers to spend three or four hours a day in the gym working on their golf muscles, but establishing a golf-specific workout regimen will not only improve your scores, it will add years to your life and make you feel better. If you won't work out for your health, do it for your golf game. Either way, you will live a healthier, happier life if you carve out a little time each day for exercise.

Why Is Strength Important?

No matter what your age, build, or sports experience, building strength through weight training is a lifestyle activity you should incorporate into your routine as surely as you plan your meals. Not only will weight lifting cut down on the amount of fat in your body, it will improve your stamina, increase your ability to concentrate, and make you stronger. As a side benefit your golf game will improve. You will hit longer, straighter tee shots, crisper, more controlled iron shots, and your short game skills will improve exponentially. Getting stronger through weight training is a no-lose proposition—one every player should take up.

Don't fall prey to that old adage about women weight lifters becoming too bulked up and losing their femininity. Unless you are already engaged in an intense workout regimen, you would have to spend six to eight hours a day in the gym lifting heavy weights and eating a lot of protein to come anywhere close to developing the kind of muscles you see on today's female bodybuilders. What you should do with weight training is decrease your body-fat percentage, strengthen bone mass, improve blood flow throughout your body, and firm and tone your figure. What's wrong with that?

Plus you improve your golf game. Strength in all areas of the body is important to better golf.

- A solid core—strong abdominal and oblique (or side) muscles—is critical to good posture and turn.

- Your shoulders, arms, and upper back muscles initiate the backswing, control the club throughout the swing, and rotate and extend the club through impact and follow-through.

- Your hamstrings, hip girdle, calf muscles, glutes, and quadriceps (or thigh muscles) generate most of the power in the swing, as well as supporting your setup and providing the firm foundation on which the swing is built.

- The lumbar (or lower back) supports the rotation of the upper body around the lower body in the backswing and unwinding of the upper body through impact. Without a strong lower back, you're susceptible to injury and fatigue in that area.

Strength Training for Better Golf

have been working out for over a decade, and every year I learn more about the muscles important to golf and how a balanced strength-training regimen can improve your game. You should seek the advice of a certified personal trainer before embarking on any serious programs, and you should always check with your doctor before making substantial lifestyle changes. Always start any weight-training program with light weights (as light as three pounds, and never any heavier than eight pounds in the beginning stages) and work yourself slowly into shape.

Never overdo it. This is not a crash course; this is a lifestyle change. Once you start, you should lift weights for the rest of your life, so pace yourself for the long haul. This is not a "Lose ten pounds in six weeks!" fad. It's a way of life that will forever affect the way you feel about yourself. Build something that will last.

■ *Squats for tighter buns.* After an adequate warm-up, you always want to start strength training by working the larger muscles first. This means starting with your lower body, your legs and glutes, and moving up to your back, then your chest, shoulders, triceps, biceps, and abs.

The first exercise I recommend can be done with or without weights. It strengthens your buns, while also working your hamstrings

My knees never pass
in front of my toes.

(the long muscles on the backs of your legs). It's called a "standing squat," and you can do it in your bedroom, living room, or office in addition to the gym. With your feet shoulder-width apart and your toes pointed slightly outward, start this exercise by bending your knees and sticking your bottom out, keeping your back straight and your head up. Bring your arms forward for balance as you slowly lower your bottom to an area just above your knees. Your weight should be in your heels as you smoothly squat into a seated position. Then you should push through your heels to bring yourself back upright. In the beginning, I recommend that you do not hold any weights.

As you get more proficient at this exercise you can add weights by simply holding dumbbells in each hand and letting your arms hang at your sides. But in the beginning, you should simply repeat this standing squat ten to twenty times. You will feel a difference in your buns and hamstrings in no time.

■ *Lunges for quad strength.* The quadriceps (commonly called the "thigh muscles") are some of the biggest and strongest in the body because they support your body weight as you walk around all day. They are also one of the most critical muscle groups in golf. Your quads support your lower body throughout the swing, play a pivotal role in the hip rotation and lower body delivery during the downswing. Without strong quadriceps, players are forced to rely on their hands and arms (smaller and weaker muscles) to swing the club through impact. But those with strong thighs (Jack Nicklaus and Nancy Lopez being the best examples) can deliver the club consistently through impact because of the solid foundation on which their swings are built.

To get the most out of your quadriceps, hold a light dumbbell in each hand and take one giant step forward, stretching your step as far

◀

Back straight, weight
on front heel.

as possible while maintaining your balance. This is the start position
for an exercise called the "lunge." From here, with your weight evenly
centered and your back perfectly straight, drop your rear knee toward
the ground, slowly lowering your body until your forward thigh is parallel to the ground. Then you should slowly rise out of the squat, focusing on the thigh muscle of the forward leg. If you repeat this exercise
ten to fifteen times per leg, then rest for about thirty seconds and perform another ten to fifteen reps per leg, you will feel substantial toning
and strengthening in your quadriceps.

Your front knee should never extend forward in this exercise. If
your front knee moves past your foot, not only are you not exercising
your quads, you could irritate your knee. To insure proper form, have a
fitness instructor watch you the first couple of times you try this exercise, and never do it without a mirror nearby to check your form.

- -

- *Adductor, or "inner thigh," squats.* Another crucial muscle group during the hip rotation of the downswing is the adductor, or inner thigh muscles. Strengthening this muscle group improves your chances of making strong, consistent swings late in the round, and it allows you to practice longer hours with greater confidence that you are still making a good lower body move throughout the swing.

   With your feet six to twelve inches wider than shoulder-width apart and your feet angled outward so that your toes are pointing at forty-five-degree angles away from your body, you start this exercise by holding the end of a dumbbell in both hands and letting your arms hang between your legs directly in front of you. Then, keeping your back straight, you bend your knees, slowly lowering your hips, simulating a plié from *Swan Lake*. Pressing through your heels, you then slowly and smoothly extend your legs back to the start position.

▶

Head up, weight
on your heels;
don't let your knees
pass your toes.

Because your adductor muscles are some of the strongest in your body anyway (because of all the time you spend using them to stand and walk), you should repeat this exercise ten to fifteen times, then take a thirty-second break before going through another set of ten to fifteen reps. When you're finished, you should feel a sense of firmness and slight fatigue in your adductor muscles, but it is also a good feeling, a strong feeling that lets you know you've gotten a good workout.

■ *Abductor, or "outer thigh," lifts*. Your abductors are the muscles that allow you to side kick, spread your legs apart, and otherwise move your legs from side to side. In golf they support the lower body as the shoulders and torso are turning on the backswing, and they help initiate the downswing by engaging the hips to rotate toward the target.

▼
A small but important strengthening motion.

They are also difficult muscles to work because the side-to-side range of motion for your legs is so small. The best exercise I've found for strengthening the abductor muscles starts with you lying on your side on the floor or on a mat. Place a dumbbell on your thigh, an inch or so above the knee of your top leg, and hold the weight in place with the hand closest to that leg. This is your start position. Now, lift your knee (and the weight) slowly, then return it to the start position.

Like the adductor muscles, the abductor muscles support your

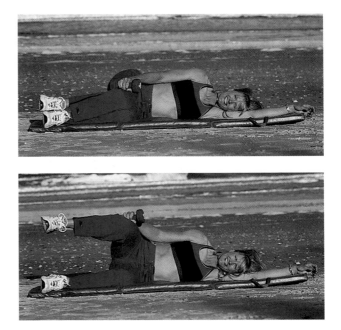

weight throughout your everyday life, so they are tough little buggers. Because of that, you should be able to repeat this lift ten to fifteen times, then rest thirty seconds and do it again.

It might take a week or so for you to feel the effects of this lift. But one day you'll say to yourself, "Hey, I've walked eighteen holes today, making good swings all day long, and my legs aren't the least bit tired." That's when you know your workout is paying off. And you'll see the difference later that day when you tally your scorecard.

■   *Toe raises for proper footwork.* That big muscle on the back of your lower leg—the one that allows you to walk and stand on your toes—is the gastrocnemius, commonly known as the calf muscle. These muscles provide the motion you need during the backswing and downswing. With them, you can make a smooth rotation of the lower body

▶

Be aware of your
balance as you
perform this exercise.

and a smooth transition from the backswing to the downswing. Without them, you would be hitting flat-footed slap shots that are going short and sideways.

The best exercise to strengthen the calf muscles is a lift called the toe raise. Starting flat-footed with dumbbells in each hand, you slowly raise up onto your toes, stopping for a two-second count at the top, then slowing lowering yourself back to a flat-footed position. The key to making this lift work is being slow and deliberate in your motion. Anybody can hop up on her toes, but by making the motion slow and smooth, you isolate and strengthen the calf muscles.

■ *Bent rows and reverse rows for the back.* The latissimus dorsi, or "lats," as they're commonly called, run just under your shoulder blades and are some of the biggest upper-body muscles involved in swinging the golf club. In addition to being an integral part of the upper body rotation during the backswing and downswing, the lat muscles also help you lift the club on plane on the backswing and keep it on plane throughout the downswing and follow-through. They are big, important golf muscles that warrant a lot of attention in your strength training.

I recommend two similar lifts to strengthen the lat muscles. One requires a bench, and the other can be done while free standing in a room. These lifts aren't interchangeable. Because the lats are such big muscles, you need two separate lifts that focus on two areas of the same muscle group, the upper and lower lat.

The first lift, known as the bent row, works the lower position of the lat muscle, the part that runs from the center of your spine to your ribcage between your shoulder blades and your hips. You start this lift with one knee on a bench and your upper body bent at the waist so that the arm opposite the elevated knee hangs straight down. Holding a dumbbell in that extended arm, you perform the exercise by slowly pulling the weight up to your torso, keeping your elbow tight against your side. Then you slowly return to the start position, and repeat for ten to fifteen reps with both arms.

Because you're alternating arms, there's no need to rest between sets in this lift. You can go from exercising your right lat muscle to exercising your left side and back to your right without stopping. One side recovers while the other is working. Two to three sets of ten to fifteen lifts, and you'll feel a difference in your upper back.

The second exercise works the upper part of the lat muscle and can be performed without a bench. This one is called the reverse row,

▼

Note how straight my back is. That's very important.

and it is done while standing bent at the waist so that your back is parallel to the ground. Your arms are hanging in front of your chest and you are holding a dumbbell in each hand so that your palms are facing outward and your knuckles are facing your thighs. From this position you slowly pull both dumbbells to your chest as if you were crewing a rowboat. Then you slowly return your arms to their extended start position and repeat the lift ten to fifteen times.

You can rest between sets of this one, but keep it short, maybe thirty seconds, then repeat the exercise. Two or three sets of this lift is a good workout. You will feel a difference in your back, and if you work at it for several months, you'll see a difference in the distance you hit your drives.

◄

Start with light
weights and slowly
work up to something
a little heavier.

■　*Reverse dips on a bench.* Immediately after doing your lat lifts, you should turn around and perform an exercise called a dip on the bench. This exercise doesn't require weights, but it's a tough one. Sitting on the bench with your hands holding on to the sides, you start this exercise by sliding your bottom off the bench, keeping your legs straight and supporting your weight with your extended arms. To execute the exercise, you slowly lower your bottom toward the floor by bending your elbows. Then you finish the exercise by pushing your body back up until your arms are straight again.

To say this is a hard exercise is an understatement. If you aren't a seasoned lifter I'll be surprised if you're able to do more than five or six dips. But don't quit! It's an important exercise in that it works your shoulders, triceps (the back of your arms), and your lat muscles at the same time. It also requires you to keep your tummy tight and your "core" mus-

▶

You won't be able
to do many of these
in the beginning,
but keep trying.

cles taut throughout. This is exactly the kind of exercise Lori Kane has in
mind when she talks about LPGA players improving their "core muscles."

■ *Chest press.* With the upper back adequately exercised, it's time
to work the opposing muscle group, the chest. This is where women
start getting skittish. All our lives we've heard that chest presses and
push-ups are somehow unladylike and that they build bulk in ways and
areas that are "unfeminine." Plus golfers aren't supposed to build their
chest muscles because it restricts the turn and makes them too tight.

I can tell you from a decade of experience that this is a load of
garbage. Good golf is about balance. If you strengthen your upper back
you have to strengthen the opposing muscle group, your chest, just as
you should strengthen your lower back along with your abdomen. To
work one without working the other puts your body out of balance,
which is terrible for your posture and even worse for your game.

You don't have to worry about building bulk in the chest region. Unless you're bench pressing twice your body weight, exercising your chest can do nothing but improve your overall strength and help you make a more fluid golf swing.

To execute the chest press, you must lie down on the bench with your chest and head facing the sky. With dumbbells in both hands, bring your arms up so that your forearms and upper arms form ninety-degree angles. Now slowly extend your arms so that the two dumbbells touch each other directly over your sternum with your arms fully extended. Once the dumbbells touch, slowly return to the start position so that the lift and return are one fluid motion, much like the swing itself.

You might not be able to complete ten to fifteen repetitions of this lift the first time you try it, but do the best you can. If you're having trouble, choose a lighter weight and get as close to the fifteen reps as possible. Then rest for thirty seconds and give it another try.

▼
Chest press.

▲

Push-ups: nose
touches the mat.

■ *Modified push-ups.* These are just like the ones you had to do in phys-ed back in junior high. With your knees on the floor, your feet in the air, and your upper body supported by your hands on the floor in front of you, slowly lower your body as far as you can without touching the floor (my coach used to make me touch my nose to the floor) then push yourself back to the start position.

Like dips, this might be one where you have a little trouble. If it's been a while since you did any sort of strength training, you might have difficulty getting past that fifth or sixth push-up, but do the best you can. If you get as high as eight or ten, you're doing great. I never recommend more than fifty push-ups at a time, but if you're a seasoned gym rat who does 100 push-ups a day, by all means continue your standard workout. It can do nothing but make you a stronger, better golfer in the long run.

■ *Front shoulder raise, lateral shoulder lift, and rear deltoid lift.* Just as the lat muscles required two separate lifts to hit every part of the muscle, the deltoid (or shoulder muscle), one of the most complex muscles in the body, has three distinct parts, each of which should be strengthened independently.

The first part of the shoulder, the "frontal deltoid," is the part of the shoulder your fingertips touch when you put your hand over your heart to say the Pledge of Allegiance. It is the part of the shoulder muscle that initiates the backswing and the part that keeps the club on plane.

The lift that strengthens this part of the shoulder is called the front shoulder raise. Sitting on the edge of the bench, hold the dumbbells in both hands with your palms down and your arms straight but resting on your legs. Keeping your arms straight, slowly lift the dumbbells until they are at eye level and your arms are extended directly in front of you. Without interrupting or speeding the motion, return to the starting position and repeat for ten to fifteen reps.

This is another one that might be tough. If you aren't accustomed to lifting with your shoulders, you should use the lightest weight you have to start out. Form is important on this lift. Too often I see people in the gym arching their backs to get the weight up. This is doing nothing for their shoulder, and it's doing a lot of damage to their backs. If you can only do five or ten reps, so be it. But never sacrifice form for more repetitions.

▼

Front shoulder raise: light weights,

The center part of the deltoid runs from the ball joint where the humerus attaches to the torso along the outside of the arm. It's the part of the shoulder those inclined to such things save for their favorite tattoos. It's also the leading shoulder muscle in the downswing, and strengthening it can vastly improve your swing speed.

Sitting in the same spot at the edge of your bench with the dumbbells in both hands and your arms at your sides, keep your arms straight and slowly raise them from your sides until you have formed a T with your body. Without pausing or

changing the rhythm of the lift, return your arms to the start position and repeat for ten to fifteen reps.

The center of your shoulder (known medically as the posterior deltoid) might be stronger than the front part of the muscle, or it might be weaker. Either way you shouldn't force the lift. If you have trouble, take a lighter weight. But don't sacrifice form. You can only build the kind of strength you need for golf with quality lifting. If your form is suffering and you're just too tired to continue, take a break and come back to this exercise later. It's better to rest and do it right another time than sacrifice form and risk an injury.

The rear deltoid is that part of the shoulder that women fret about, the part where we think unsightly fat is gathering, and the part we check out in the mirror every time we wear a sleeveless top. It's also the part that drives the club through impact and the part that absorbs the shock (however minor) when club hits ball and turf.

▶
Lateral shoulder
lift: arms and torso
form a T.

To strengthen this part of the shoulder requires you to kneel on your bench with your arm extended in the same way you start your lat pulls. With your arms slightly bent but maintaining a consistent angle throughout, lift your elbow up until your upper arm is parallel with the ground. Then slowly return to the start position and repeat ten to fifteen times with both arms. Since you're alternating arms for this lift, there's no need to rest between sets. You should alternate arms until you have completed two sets of ten to fifteen reps with each shoulder.

▲

Rear deltoid lift: one arm at a time.

■ *Triceps kickbacks and overhead extensions*. The triceps are the muscles that run along the backs of your arms, the ones that allow you to push a shopping cart, and the ones that keep your arms extended throughout the golf swing, creating separation and arc. It's the biggest and strongest muscle in your arm, and it requires a couple of strengthening exercises.

The first is called the kickback. With one knee on the bench, your torso parallel to the floor, and the opposite arm hanging at your side holding a dumbbell (the same position you were in for the lat pull and the rear deltoid lift), start the lift by bending the elbow so that the fore-

▲

Triceps kickback: fully
extend the arm.

arm and upper arm form a ninety-degree angle and the upper arm is
parallel with the ground. Then complete the lift by "kicking" the weight
out, extending the arm outward until it is straight, and the entire arm is
parallel with the ground. Without pausing or changing the speed of your
lift, return the weight by bending the elbow back to a ninety-degree

▶

Overhead extensions:
light weight, good form.

angle and repeat the exercise ten to fifteen times with each arm, rotating until you complete two sets with both your left and right triceps.

The second triceps exercise is called an overhead extension. From a seated position, lift one dumbbell over your head, holding it with both hands. Then slowly drop the weight behind your head by bending at the elbows. Without stopping, and keeping your elbows close to your ears, complete the lift by extending your arms and lifting the weight back over your head. Do this ten to fifteen times, rest thirty seconds, then do it again.

■   *Simultaneous biceps curls and single-arm hammer curls.* The opposing muscle to the triceps is the biceps, the muscle that runs along the inside of your arm between your elbow and your shoulder and the one that allows you to pick up your coffee cup every morning. The biceps muscles lift the club during the backswing and help you hold your L through the downswing. They also look great when properly toned. I love seeing a student who has strong biceps. I know she cares about her body and isn't afraid of a little work to get herself in shape.

The biceps are strengthened by a lift known in the health industry as a "curl." There are a couple of ways to execute the curl, and I recommend you alternate between the two. The first is called a simultaneous curl. Holding dumbbells in both hands with your arms extended, contract your arms by bending your elbows, bringing the weights up to your shoulders with your palms facing your body. Then slowly return the weight to the start position by extending your arms. You should repeat this lift ten to fifteen times.

For your second set, I recommend you change things up a bit. Rotate your hands so that you are holding the dumbbells as you would two golf clubs (or hammers) with your arms at slight angles away from

Slow and easy: focus
on the biceps, not the
shoulders and back.

the center of your body. Now, using one arm at a time, curl the weight so that the head of the dumbbell touches the front of your shoulder. Repeat this exercise ten to fifteen times with each arm. You should feel a difference between the two lifts in the area of the biceps you work. Both are great for your golf game, and they won't hurt your looks either.

Frequency

See if this sounds familiar: You wake up one morning—usually right after the holidays when the smell of turkey and raspberry chutney still permeates your hallways—and you're stunned by the grotesque creature greeting you in the bathroom mirror. "How could I have let myself go like this?" you ask. "What did I do to become this unsightly?"

Depressed by your postholiday spread, you resolve to get back in shape. Maybe you join a gym or get a three-visit guest pass to the local Y or simply dust off the dumbbells that have been stuffed in the closet for decades. Whatever route you take, you probably jump into your new workout ritual with great gusto.

The next morning, everything hurts but your hair. After a week or so, you forgo the pain and forget about the commitment, resigning yourself to a little pudge here and there.

It doesn't have to be that way. Strength training is not a race. It's a slow, steady lifestyle change, but the payoff is immeasurable. You will look better, feel better, have more energy, better concentration and, as an added bonus, play better golf.

That is often the key that unlocks the door to fitness. I've taught a lot of students whose only visits to the gym were walk-throughs on their way to the tanning bed. But once I explained the tangible benefits of strength training on their golf games, these players became semidedicated weight lifters. Nebulous benefits like longer life, lower cholesterol, and added energy didn't excite these people. The thought of gaining twenty extra yards off the tee and hitting a 5-iron instead of a 5-wood into a nasty little par-three had them giggling like teenagers as they signed up for two-year gym memberships.

But strength training isn't an everyday thing. Unlike cardiovascular training or stretching, muscles that have been fatigued through weight lifting need at least forty-eight hours to recover. That's why you should never do the same lifts two days in a row.

I divide my weight lifting workout into three sections. On day one, I work my biceps and back muscles; day two is devoted to triceps, chest, and shoulders, and day three is legs and lower body. By day four, my biceps and back have had a chance to recover, so I start the rotation over again. You might find a different system, which is fine as long as you work every muscle group at least twice a week.

You can also scrap the myth that you can't lift weights and play golf the same day. Tiger Woods does it all the time. Even Senior PGA Tour players like Larry Nelson, Hale Irwin, and Hubert Green—no young spry lads are they—lift weights with a personal trainer during tournament weeks. It's the norm among pros these days. You should make it a part of your normal routine as well.

Ab Work—
The Everyday Workout

While your muscles need a break to recover from weight lifting, the "core" muscles of your abdominal region can stand a hearty workout every single day. I usually start my mornings with between 500 and 700 crunches and various isolation exercises to work the lower abs and oblique muscles (the muscles on your sides, where love handles can gather if you aren't careful).

It's taken me a long time to reach this level of proficiency in my ab workouts, but the payoff has been extraordinary. I can hit hundreds of golf balls a day without fear of back problems because I've taken the time and put forth the effort to strengthen my core. I can also stretch back and go after a shot hard (a no-no for most players) without fear of losing my balance and hitting a wild sideways shot. I couldn't do this if I weren't strong throughout my midsection. Conditioned abs give me the support and confidence I need to be aggressive on the course.

Nancy Lopez says she does 500 crunches a day, while Annika is up to 1,000. Granted, these women are conditioned athletes who have been at this awhile, but if you can do fifty or 100 a day, you gain a tremendous competitive advantage over your peers who don't work out at all.

Some beginning abdominal work I recommend for my students includes:

- *Lower ab raises.* This can be done on a bench or even a chair in your office. Sitting on the edge of the bench, hold yourself in place with your hands and slide your bottom off the edge. Then, with your knees slightly flexed raise one leg up as high as you can and slowly return it

----

▶

Lower ab raises.

to the floor. If you repeat this twenty-five to thirty times with each leg you should feel it in your lower abdominal region, that hard-to-reach area below your navel.

▼

Pedaling the bike.

■ *Riding the imaginary bike.* When I was a child, Jack La Lanne had the only fitness show on television. It was considered an odd curiosity at the time, a well-built guy in tights leading calisthenics on TV in the morning. Now we know Jack was ahead of his time.

One of his favorite exercises thirty years ago is still one of the best lower abdominal exercises you can do. Lying on your back, simply lift your legs into the air and peddle an imaginary bike. Make big rotations with your feet and legs, but remain smooth and fluid. If you do this for five to ten minutes you will feel a change in your lower abdominal region. And if you ride this bike every day, you'll see a change in your waistline.

- *Standard industrial crunch.* For a full ab workout that hits everything from your belt to your sternum, there's nothing like the good ol'-fashioned crunch. Lying on your back with your legs bent and your knees and feet in the air, put your hands behind your head and try to touch your chin to your knees. Your legs will pull inward and your shoulder blades will lift off the floor as you "crunch" your body, contracting every muscle in the abdominal region in this one exercise.

You might only be able to do ten of these the first few times you try, but don't get discouraged. If you make crunches a part of your daily routine, it won't be long before you're surprising yourself.

- *Cross lateral oblique crunch.* This exercise attacks the love-handle region of your sides, which also happens to be the muscle that allows your shoulders to follow your hips into the downswing. Lying on your back with your legs bent, the same position you were in for the standard industrial crunch, lock your hands behind your head and

touch your left elbow to your right knee. Then return to the start position and touch your right elbow to your left knee.

This crossing-over-the-body action works a muscle you might not have exercised in years, so don't be surprised if you have some trouble cranking out the reps on this one. No matter how poorly you do in the beginning, stick to it. You will improve and you will see the results in your performance on the course.

Stretching the Golf Muscles

Strength is only one part of the golf-fitness equation. The other critical element in training your muscles for golf is flexibility and pliability. Stiff muscles and tendons inhibit your setup and cause you to slouch, impede and shorten your backswing, force you to lift and throw the club, and squelch any chance you might have to make a fluid turn of the hips through impact. You cannot generate clubhead speed if your upper body muscles are stiff and drawn, and you can't make solid contact if you're too stiff to turn.

That's why every professional golfer, regardless of the workout regimen, spends a half hour to an hour a day stretching. You can't go into a locker room on any tour without seeing someone engaged in a stretch, and the fitness trailers and hotel gymnasiums at tour sites are filled with personal trainers assisting players with their stretching exercises. It's uniformly accepted on tour: You can't play if you don't stretch.

Unlike tour pros, most of my students, male and female, don't have an hour before they play to stretch and another hour to hit balls, roll putts, and warm up their swings for a round. They're lucky if they get their golf shoes tied before rolling up to the first tee.

I'd love to give my students a full complement of stretching exercises, but I know they're more likely to ride jumpseat on the space shuttle than they are to spend adequate time stretching. But there are some stretches every golfer can and should do before every round.

■ *Hamstring stretch.* This stretch, designed for the back of your leg, also loosens some of the muscles of your lumbar or lower back. Keeping your leg straight, put your heel on the bumper of your golf cart and slowly lean forward by tilting at the hips. Lower your upper body until you feel the stretch in your hamstring. Then hold that stretch for thirty seconds, and repeat with both legs.

▲

You can stretch your hamstrings anywhere.

Never, ever, bounce a stretch, and never rush into or out of a stretch. Bouncing stretches causes more injuries than anything else in our game. Slowly enter a stretch; hold it there for thirty seconds (the

minimum time required for a stretch to be effective), then slowly return to the start position.

- *Quadriceps stretch.* The opposing muscle to the hamstring is the quadriceps, and stretching it is fairly straightforward and easy. Holding on to the edge of your cart or a wall or even just your club for support, bend one knee and grab your shoelaces with the opposite hand. Now slowly pull on your foot until you feel the stretch of the large thigh muscle in the front part of your leg. To increase this stretch, tilt forward slightly from the waist. Hold this stretch for thirty seconds and repeat with both legs.

- *Calf and Achilles stretch.* With your legs warming up from the preceding stretches, it's time for one of my favorites. Propping your toe up on the tire of your golf cart and grabbing the cart brackets for support, slowly apply weight to the propped foot and lean forward until you feel a stretch in your calf muscle and your Achilles tendon just above the ankle. This stretch feels great! After you hold this one for thirty seconds with each leg, you feel like you could jump over your cart and sprint down the first fairway.

▲
Slowly move in and out of all stretches.

◄

Lateral oblique
stretch: one of the
most important and
often overlooked
stretches in golf.

■ *Lateral oblique stretch.* Moving up to the trunk, the first stretch I
recommend requires you to hold a golf club directly over your head
with one hand on the grip and the other on the head or the hosel. From
this position you should slowly lean to one side, keeping your feet firmly
planted and keeping your head centered between your arms. You'll feel
this stretch from your rib cage to your hip. Hold it for thirty seconds
and slowly return to the start position and repeat on the other side.

■ *Torso stretch.* Now it's time to stretch the trunk muscles you will
be twisting and turning throughout your round. Placing a club behind
you and across your shoulders while holding the grip in one hand and
the hosel in the other, you should assume the posture you would use
to hit a shot—feet shoulder-width apart, knees flexed, bowing at the
waist with your back straight—and rotate your shoulders as though you
are making a backswing. Turn as far as you can and hold that position

► Hold this torso stretch to widen your turn.

▼ Chest and shoulder stretch using a golf cart.

for thirty seconds. Then slowly unwind and go to your finish position and hold it for thirty seconds.

The temptation to bounce or run through this one quickly can be overwhelming, but don't succumb. Those players you see on the range running through this exercise in five or six seconds aren't stretching their muscles and could be doing damage to themselves. You might spend a longer amount of time in this stretch than any of your playing partners, but the added time will be worth it.

■ *Chest and shoulder stretch.* Using the brackets on your golf cart or the frame of a doorway, extend both arms and grab the bracket. Then lean forward until you feel the stretch in your chest and shoulders. Hold that stretch for thirty seconds. To increase the stretch, move your feet closer to the cart and increase the angle of your lean.

■ *Triceps stretch.* This one is easy, and it feels great. Standing straight up, reach over your head and try to touch your spine as far down your back as you can. When you've reached as far as you can, place your other hand on your elbow and gently press the arm back a little farther until you feel the stretch in your triceps. Hold this stretch the obligatory thirty seconds, then repeat with the other arm.

■ *Neck stretch.* The final preround stretch I recommend is the one that gives you the best feeling before heading off the first tee. Standing erect, drop your chin to your chest, and gently press your head down until you feel the muscles of your neck stretch. Hold that stretch for thirty seconds, then tilt your head from side to side, stretching each area of the neck for thirty seconds.

You'll feel this one all the way down your back. And when you're done, you'll be amazed how much better you feel setting up over that first shot of the day.

▲
Triceps stretches require no equipment.

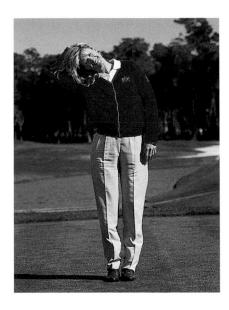

Cardio Training

Asking most golfers to run or jog or bike or take aerobics classes is usually like asking a cat to sprout wings and fly. It's a noble thought, but it's not going to happen. I like to think my students are different. If you've gone to the effort of establishing a strength program and you're committed to stretching every day, not adding a cardiovascular component to your workout is foolhardy. You're two-thirds of the way there. You might as well complete the golf-fitness cycle by running, walking, jogging, cycling, working on the stair machine, or taking an aerobics class for at least twenty minutes every day.

As I've tried to pound home in the previous pages, golf is a game of rhythm and timing. Out-of-shape golfers with racing heartbeats and fatigued muscles can't make the same smooth, rhythmic swings they did when they stepped onto the first tee and their bodies were fresh. Well-conditioned athletes don't have that problem. They get stronger as the round progresses. The added blood flow you gain from good cardiovascular conditioning also improves your elasticity and your concentration. A healthy body does, indeed, translate into a sharp, healthy mind.

You've worked too hard to improve your game to ignore this critical element. Getting in cardiovascular shape is as important to golf as any swing mechanic or short game drill. Take it seriously and you'll see dramatic improvements in your scores.

ONE OF THE REASONS I've found that women have a high degree of anxiety about golf is their self-perceived ignorance of the rules. I'm not talking about the rules of play—those you can easily find by reading *The Rules of Golf*—but the unwritten rules of decorum, etiquette, and generally accepted conduct. You won't find these rules posted on the bulletin board, and there is no Emily Post to guide you through the minefield of common-law practices in golf. Most of these lessons are learned by trial and error, and it's the *error* part that frightens a lot of women.

13 Unwritten Rules of the Game

I was at a cocktail party not long ago where a number of high-powered business executives were chatting about their golf games and the happenings on the professional tours from the previous weeks. They invited me to join their conversation and I did so without hesitation. What stunned me was the fact that a woman I knew, someone I had coached and whom I knew to be a fair player, stood by silently, even though engaging in this conversation would have been good for her socially and politically.

"Why didn't you jump into that discussion?" I later asked.

"I don't know," she said. "Those men didn't want to hear my opinion."

"How do you know?" I said. "You know more about golf than anybody in that group. They'll never know how much you know unless you tell them. The game gave you a great opportunity to open some doors. You shouldn't pass up those chances when you get them."

"You're right," she said. "I'll remember next time."

This woman's reluctance is not unusual. I see it all the time. Women feel like they make enough mistakes with their swings. They don't want to compound the discomfort by making some social faux pas where golf is concerned. I tell most of my students that this fear is more imagined than real. Most men who talk about the game in social settings can't hit the ball out of their shadows when they're on the course. Women shouldn't feel intimidated when it comes to joining the party. You belong in this game. Don't hesitate to show your stuff in public.

Know Your Golf Etiquette

As I've probed the question of why women aren't comfortable expressing their golf knowledge, I've discovered that many of our inhibitions stem from the stereotypes thrust upon us by centuries of male dominance in the sport. You've heard them, just as I have. "Women play too slow." "Women have no business playing the weekends." "Women should either take it seriously or give up the game." On and on these boorish critics go, flaunting their ignorance and prejudices without a hint of shame.

The best way to combat these bigots is to beat them at their own game. I'm not talking about winning on the scorecard, which is an added bonus if you become good enough. The silver bullet to kill the stereotype once and for all is for women to become more savvy about the etiquette of the game than their male critics. Once you become proficient in the subtleties of golf protocol, you can travel confidently in this game and hush the boors once and for all.

Some tips for staying in bounds when it comes to golf's unwritten rules of etiquette include:

- *Playing badly isn't a crime; playing slowly is.* Always keep up with the group ahead of you. If there isn't a group ahead of you, play at a pace that sets the standard for the rest of the groups that day. The rule of thumb in America is that an uninterrupted eighteen-hole round should take no more than four hours. The Europeans consider a four-hour round to be criminally slow. Laura Davies can play eighteen holes in a little over two hours if she's in the first group. Trish Johnson, another of Great Britain's more successful women professionals, plays so fast you have to pay attention in order to keep up with her.

No one expects amateur women to play as quickly as Laura and Trish, but you should learn to set a good pace. If there is a group in front of you, keep up with them. If there is no one ahead of you, but a group behind you is playing faster than you, wave them up at a convenient spot, step aside, and let them play through. Set and keep a good pace, and you will have few problems on the course.

This doesn't mean you should sacrifice your own game for the sake of getting off the golf course quickly. I was playing with a woman student of mine recently who found herself stuck in a sand trap and unable to get out. After three tries, she picked up her ball and said, "I'm going to stop. I don't want to hold anybody up." This would have been a fine thing to say if there was a group behind us. But not only was there no one on the hole behind us, we were the only people on the golf course!

"Who are you worrying about holding up?" I said. "We're the only people on the golf course. If you want to pick up on this hole, fine. But there's nobody else out here, and I've got all day. Enjoy yourself."

Learning to set a good pace is something all women (and men) should do early and often in golf. But don't fall victim to unnecessary "I don't want to hold anybody up" anxieties.

■ *Be ready to hit when it's your turn.* Golf has an honor system that determines the order of play. On the first tee, the first player to hit is chosen by lot. You flip a coin, throw a tee, draw straws, or simply agree on an order at the first hole. From that point forward, the player who wins the hole is said to have the "honor" on the next tee. If everyone ties (or halves) the hole, the honor from the previous hole carries forward. In the fairway and on the green things get a little more complicated. The person who is farthest away from the hole, be it in the rough, the fairway, the bunker, or on the green, is said to be "away" and therefore has the honor. Sometimes it's tough to see who's away, especially if your ball is on one side of the fairway and your playing partner is in the rough on the other side, but in those cases, you work out the honor with your friends.

The most important part of the order of play is to be ready when it's your turn to hit. There's nothing more frustrating to an accomplished player than to watch a partner who sits in the golf cart while everyone else hits, then, when it's her turn to play, she slowly crawls out of the seat, puts on her glove, fiddles around with her golf bag, checks the yardage, wind, and lie before taking a club out of the bag. This is usually followed by three or four practice swings (one is preferred, two is the max), and another fifteen to twenty waggles before any attempt to hit the shot is made. By this time the rest of the group is pulling their hair out.

Such behavior is rude and shouldn't be tolerated in golf. Choose your club and walk to your ball before it's your time to hit. If your ball is in someone else's line of play, stand to the side so you don't distract

▼

Don't wait until it's your turn to hit to put on your gloves or clean your clubs.

your playing partner, but stay close enough to your ball so you can move into position when it's your turn to hit. Have your yardage measured, analyze your lie, and know what kind of shot you are about to play while others around you are playing their shots. When it's your turn, be ready to hit. It doesn't matter how well you play, as long as you respect others around you by not wasting time.

■   *Be mindful of where you park the golf cart, trolley, or golf bag.* There are enough obstacles on the golf course. You don't need to add another one by parking your cart, or trolley, or plopping your golf bag in your own or someone else's line of play. In addition to being inconsider-

▼

Park your cart behind the green.

ate, this can be dangerous. A ball ricocheting off a golf cart or bag can do damage to your equipment and to anyone standing nearby.

You should also be mindful of the group behind you. If you've hit your ball onto the green or in the fringe near the green, you can either pull your cart or trolley behind the green or leave it in front of the green and walk up to play your shot. The only problem with the latter option is that walking back to retrieve your cart slows down the group behind you. After you putt out, walking behind the green to your equipment allows the group waiting behind you to go ahead and play. Plus, you'll find the average time of your round is cut by as much as thirty to thirty-five percent if you simply park your equipment behind the green before you putt.

■ *Observe etiquette for attending the pin.* It's against the rules to hit the flagstick with a shot played from the putting green. That means that if you're on the green, you need to remove the flag from the hole. The only problem is that some putts are so long that you can't see the hole. In those cases a friend, caddie, or fellow player "attends" the flagstick. This person stands next to the hole and holds the pin while you putt. After the ball is rolling toward the hole, the attendee removes the flagstick.

Sometimes you need to attend the pin for the other players in your group. On those occasions you should approach the hole without walking through the line of anyone's putt, then stand to the side of the hole so your feet don't block the player's view of her line and make sure your shadow isn't encroaching on the hole or the intended line of the putt.

You should also hold the flag itself so that it doesn't flap in the breeze, and twist the flagstick slightly, partially removing it from the hole before the player putts. There have been many instances where a flagstick has gotten stuck in the hole, and the person attending the pin was unable to pull it out in time. This happened to Arnold Palmer during a *Shell's Wonderful World of Golf* match, a made-for-television event with Arnold playing Jack Nicklaus at the World Golf Village course they designed together. Arnold's caddie that week happened to be his architectural partner, Ed Seay. A great golf-course architect but not a professional caddie, Ed was attending the flag for Arnold. When Arnold hit his putt Ed yanked and pulled on the flagstick to no avail. It was stuck. As Arnold's ball rolled closer to the hole, Ed gave the pin one giant gasping pull, and the entire cup came up out of the ground. The only thing that saved Arnold from losing the hole, and Ed from being fired on the spot from any future caddy duties, was the fact that Arnold missed the putt. That didn't stop Arnold and Jack from ribbing Ed the remainder of that round and for days thereafter. Don't be bashful about attending the flagstick, but don't be confused either. A player can have the flag attended only when the ball is on the green. If the ball is off the putting surface, even if it's only by an inch or two, the flagstick has to remain either in or out of the hole. If you're closer to the hole than your playing partner is, volunteer to remove the flagstick, or hold it while the other players in your group putt. Once everyone agrees that the flagstick should be removed, take it away from the hole and lay it on the ground (preferably in the fringe) so that it's not in any player's line of play or sight line. If you're the first player to hole out, retrieve the flagstick and be ready to return it the hole when everyone is through putting. This saves a few extra seconds on each green, which can quicken your overall round by as much as fifteen minutes.

■   *Watch your step.* Putting is another part of the game that's hard enough as it is. Any add-on impediments are unwanted. A footprint is one such avoidable obstacle. It's hard enough to read the speed and break of a putt and make a solid stroke. An indentation in the green from someone's foot is enough to push you over the edge.

It's common courtesy to walk around the edge of the green so as not to accidentally step in the path of a companion's putt. You should also be aware of something called the "through line," that line behind the hole that a ball might travel if it misses the cup. Players are conscious of both their line and their through line. If you tap dance through either, it's a serious breach of etiquette.

■   *Be shadow-conscious.* Former NFL running back Marcus Allen has been a student of mine for years. He's improved a lot since we first starting working together, but one hang-up Marcus still has is swinging when his shadow is over the ball. He can be playing the best golf of his life and the minute his shadow creeps over the ball he shanks it. I tell him to focus on his target, but he says, "I can't, Cindy. When I see my shadow swing the club back, my eyes have to follow it." After watching him shank four or five shots with his shadow in his line, I said, "Marcus, you're just going to have to play all your golf in Seattle."

If Marcus's own shadow presents such a problem, imagine what someone else's shadow in his line or on his ball might do to his game. If you're playing with friends, be cognizant of your shadow. You should never cast a shadow over another player's ball nor should you let your shadow encroach onto the line of someone else's putt. This can get tough late in the day when shadows lengthen, but it's a common courtesy in golf—one you would be well served to learn and follow.

▶

Don't let your
shadow intrude on
someone's line.

- *Chat between shots, but show respect for others.* It's awfully annoying to go through your preshot routine, set up, waggle the golf club, then have to step away and start the process over because somebody in your group picked that moment to share a story about the neighbor's Yorkie and some nearby azaleas. Socializing is an important part of golf. But you have to show respect for those around you. When a player is into her routine, it's expected that others in the group will stand quietly until she plays her shot. You don't want others telling jokes during your backswing, so you should show the same courtesy to those around you.

    Also, unless you're an on-call physician, turn off your phone and pager on the course. Allowing those devices to interrupt your game is a disservice to your golf and insulting to others in your group.

- *Forget what you've seen on TV.* If you're a fan of television golf, you've probably seen pros take their time studying every aspect of a shot—throwing grass clippings in the air, laboring over club selection, and examining the line of a putt from every angle several times. What you don't see, and what television commentators don't emphasize enough, is that these pros have specific reasons for taking so much time over their shots. Sometimes the galleries, walking scorers, reporters, and television crews are moving around after a group leaves a hole. Players in the fairway have to wait for all that movement to stop before playing their shots. Also, tour pros try to get into a rhythm so that they aren't waiting on the group ahead of them. Once the pace of play is established pros take the time they need in order to keep moving without pushing the group ahead. If a group of tour pros falls behind, a tour official warns them to pick up the pace or face a penalty, just like the marshal at your local club.

What you rarely see on TV is how fast the first group of professionals on the course plays when they don't have any distractions or holdups. I've seen tour pros play eighteen-hole competitive rounds in less than two hours when they're in the first group. Unfortunately, TV never captures those rounds. By the time the cameras come on, the leaders are teeing off, the course is full, and play has ground to a slow crawl.

Don't let the images you see on Sunday telecasts dictate how you play, and don't be fooled into believing that good golf equals slow golf. Pros play quickly when nobody else is around. You should too.

Get Comfortable in Your Clothes and in Your Skin

Golf is an individual sport. There are no uniforms, no team logos, no rules about hair length or the color of your cap. Most clubs do set dress code standards to keep players from showing up in cut-off blue jeans or thong bikinis, but other than those few minimum standards, golfers are left on their own in terms of fashion and comfort.

That's why I'm amazed at how badly so many women golfers dress. It's as if, in an effort to fit in on the golf course, women feel they must dress like men. You've seen them. They wear baggy collared golf shirts in dark earth tones and long, pleated cotton shorts or khaki slacks. They even pull their baseball caps down over their eyes as if they are trying to hide their gender from the golfing world.

This is my biggest soapbox. Women shouldn't feel inhibited about showing their femininity and sense of fashion on the golf course. Look at players like Laura Diaz, Natalie Gulbis, and Beth Bauer. They're fantastic players who look great on the golf course. You should follow their lead. If you want to play golf in a sundress because you like the way it looks, by all means do it. If you have matching earrings and a hat, wear them. Looking good on the golf course is a virtue, not a vice. Show some originality and wear the things that make you feel comfortable on the golf course.

Some keys to getting comfortable in your clothes and in your skin include:

- *Pick clothing that gives you freedom of movement.* Loose-fitting clothing doesn't have to be baggy and unattractive. I love playing in sundresses because they are pretty and give me plenty of room to swing. Sleeveless tops and skirts are another favorite of mine. They look good and don't inhibit my range of motion.

  Some teenagers and college players have even introduced halters to the course. I'm undecided on that fashion statement, but I applaud their spunkiness for trying something new. If it's decent, attractive, and doesn't restrict your golf swing, I say give it a try.

- *Keep room for the essentials.* You don't need to carry much onto the golf course, but you do need to have room in your outfits for the few essentials you must carry. Having a pocket for a ball, a divot tool, and a few tees is a good idea. It doesn't have to be a big blousy pocket in a pair of baggy shorts. You aren't trying to cram a dozen balls and a hundred tees into your pockets. Something small and discreet will do nicely.

  You also need a place to put your glove when you take it off. If I'm wearing a skirt, I usually fold the fingers of my glove over the palm and stick it in the back waistband of the skirt. If I'm wearing a dress, I fold it in half and put it in a small pocket. And if I'm wearing shorts or slacks I put my glove in my back pocket so that a small portion of the glove protrudes out. That makes it easy to retrieve the glove after I've putted.

  You can take my advice on this front or be creative and come up with alternatives of your own. Just be aware of the essentials you have to carry and plan your wardrobe accordingly.

- *The truth about hats.* I'm in the sun for eight to ten hours a day, every day. If I didn't wear a hat my skin would turn to leather, and I would increase my risk of cancer. I'm not willing to do either, so I have a large collection of wide-brimmed hats that I wear all the time. They've become something of a signature for me. I have a hat for every outfit and every occasion, and I wear them proudly.

For safety's sake, I suggest you wear a hat at all times on the golf course. Even if you're convinced you look terrible in hats, there are so many options available these days that I'm sure you can find something that fits your needs and your tastes.

- *Have fun with it.* There's a woman who plays at my club in Florida who wears some of the most stunning outfits I've ever seen on the golf course. She is always dressed to the nines when she arrives, complete with makeup and accessories. Because of her fashion sense, she's the talk of the staff. None of the professionals at my club know a thing about this woman's golf game, but they can't wait to see her when she arrives because of what she wears.

You can create just as much buzz at your club if that's what you want to do. Have fun with the game, even when it comes to what you wear to the course. You'll get a lot more enjoyment out of your golf experience.

MY PARTING ADVICE to anyone taking up the game is to stick with it, stay the course, continue to practice, play, take lessons, learn, and enjoy the game's high points and low points. If you expect continuous improvement, a steady, unending upward climb through golf's hierarchy, you're in for a rude awakening and a future filled with consternation.

Growth in golf is a bit like growth in a child; it comes in spurts. You will make dramatic improvements in the first few months. If you practice and follow your instructor's advice you'll get better in a hurry. This will give you great hope. You'll fall in love with the game and wonder what all the fuss is about. "It's not that tough," you'll say to yourself. "I can't imagine why so many people get so upset." Then you'll

Epilogue
Staying the Course

hit your first real funk, a plateau of sorts where you can't seem to improve, lose your touch, and wonder how something that seemed so easy only a week ago could now be as foreign as cricket or curling.

This is where a lot of women call it a day. They think that because they aren't improving right away, they'll never get any better. They believe they've peaked, and there's nowhere else to go. A lot of them become frustrated and confused. They throw up their hands and say, "What's the point?"

The message I give to all my students who reach this plateau and wonder if they will ever get out of it is: Yes, you'll get better, but it might take a while. When you work your way out of this stall, you'll see another healthy spurt of improvement. You'll gain confidence again, hit good shots, build your esteem on the improved scores you are posting, and lull yourself into another false sense of security. Then the next slump will come like a bad cold at Christmas.

Hopefully you'll be more prepared for the pitfalls of your golf plateau the second time around. By then you know the frustrations that are coming, and you know that if you stay the course, continue to work, and remember the fundamentals of your game, you'll work your way out of this one too.

Golf is about fun, friendship, competition, commonality, and about being outside in the fresh air and sunshine. Some take the game on as a crusade. For them the anguish runs deep, but the highs are heavenly. Others want nothing more than a day outdoors with green grass beneath their feet and good company by their side. For them, a good shot isn't anything to get too excited about, and a bad shot is no big deal. It's only golf, after all.

No matter where you fall along golf's spectrum, I hope you will stick with the game for the long term. It is, truly, the game of a lifetime, the only sport you can enjoy from age nine to age ninety, where mothers can play with daughters, and daughters can play with granddads; a game you can, at once, love and embrace, revile and curse, but one you must never walk away from.

As you finish this book and embark on your career as a golfer, I want to you make a pledge to yourself. It goes as follows:

CINDY'S FRONT-NINE PLEDGE

1. I vow not to quit, no matter how much I dislike this game at times.

2. I pledge to practice some aspect of golf every day, even if it's nothing more than gripping a club in my office or taking a few swings in front of the bathroom mirror.

3. I will take lessons on a regular basis—no fewer than ten in the next twelve months from a pro I like and one I feel comfortable following.

4. I will hit practice balls at least as often as I play, and I will schedule time in my hectic week to hit a bucket of balls.

5. I will become a better putter through hard work at home and at the course.

6. I vow to build a better golf body by working out at home or in the gym and getting myself in shape for the game and for life.

7. I pledge to introduce one new player to the game of golf this year.

8. I will make at least ten new friends or business contacts through golf this year.

9. I vow to stay the course, to continue working and playing at golf no matter how frustrated and discouraged I might become. And I pledge to learn something about myself, about others, and about the world every day I spend playing, practicing, and loving the game.

    Now, let's get out there and have some fun!

Index

abdomen, abdominals (abs), 252, 253,
    261, 262, 273–76
abductors, 257–58
adductors, 256–57
advice, free, 29–30
alignment, 130–35
  with ball below feet, 214
  in downhill lies, 211
  in lob shot, 152
  in power fade, 206
  in practice, 63–64
  in swing, 130, 173
  in uphill lies, 209, 210
Allen, Marcus, 23–24, 37, 291
Arizona State University, 3
auditory learning, 25–26
Augusta National, 196

back
  in backswing, 252
  strength training for, 253, 259–61,
    262, 272
  stretch for, 277–78
backspin, 188
backswing, 173–82
  biceps in, 269
  club laid off on, 20–21
  deltoid in, 265
  extended, 198
  with fairway woods, 204

  with irons, 201
  lats in, 252, 259
  lower back in, 252
  outer thigh lifts for, 257
  in power fade, 206
  stretching for, 276
  toe raises for, 258–59
  waggle and, 171
  with weighted club, 195
Baena, Marisa, 249
bag, golf, 288–89
balance
  in downhill lies, 212
  drill for, 197
  importance of, 262
  in lunges, 255
  in squats, 254
  in swing, 188, 191–95, 273
  in toe raises, 258
Ballesteros, Seve, 139
ball(s)
  above feet, 212–13
  abutting fringe, 216–17
  behind the, 132–34
  below feet, 213–15
  distance from, 85
  in divot, 215
  in draw, 207
  eliminating, 193–94
  hitting farther, 197–98

ball(s) *(continued)*
  hooking, 226
  pitch shot and, 145, 146
  plastic, 194
  position, 83–84, 126–29, 142, 146, 151,
    203, 209, 210
  in power fade, 207
  practice, 136
  price of, 39
  as repackaged rejects, 43
  in sand play, 157–59
  scooping the, 186
  setup and, 114
  squeezing a, 111–12
  straight and high, 165–70
  stripe of, 203
  topspin on, 186
Baltimore Senior Classic, 80
Barkley, Charles, 37, 51
Bauer, Beth, 294
Baugh, Laura, 36, 198
Bell, Judy, 34
Beman, Deane, 155–56
bent rows, 259–60
Berg, Patty, 90, 102
Berry, Rick, 37
best-ball match, 240–41
biceps, 253, 269–71, 272
bicycle, imaginary, 274–75
birdie, 64, 224, 226, 235, 239, 242
blasts, 157–62
bogeys
  high-risk shots and, 136, 224, 226,
    228
  in match play, 239
  in points-system competition,
    242
  poor drive or approach shot and,
    64
  see also double bogeys
Bonds, Barry, 3
Brandon, Lee, 56
breasts, 121–22
British Amateur, 240
Brokaw, Tom, 37
Bush, Barbara, 34

Calcavecchia, Mark, 77
calf muscles, 252, 258–59, 278
cardio training, 282
Casper, Billy, 90
chest, 253, 262–63, 272, 280–81
China, golf in, 37–38
chip shot, 58, 136, 138–45
  on ball below feet, 214
  bunker and, 159
  difficult, 223
  flop and, 155
  on fringe ball, 217
  lob and, 152
  pitch and, 147, 148
  practice time on, 71
  in up-and-down drill, 64
clothing, 45, 294–96
club(s), 223–26
  alignment and, 63–64, 130–32, 133,
    134
  in backswing, 198
  with ball above feet, 212, 213
  with ball abutting fringe, 216–17
  with ball below feet, 214, 215
  ball position and, 126–29
  customized, 46
  distance and, 230–32
  in divot, 215–16
  in downhill lies, 211, 212
  in draw, 207
  to hips, 134
  K, 120–21
  "laid off," 20, 175, 180, 181
  lofted, 217
  mirror and, 60
  moving off with, 55
  in one-more-club game, 237–38
  picking, 139–41, 221
  in power fade, 206
  purchase of, 4, 39, 40–46
  for recovery shots, 218, 219–20, 221
  rotating, 112
  in sand play, 158, 160–62
  in shot diary, 232–33
  shots with, 138, 139–41, 142, 143, 151,
    206

sweet spot and, 197
in uphill lie, 210
weighted, 195
see also grip; swing; *specific kinds of clubs*
"coil" approach, 179, 182
competition, 3, 4, 5, 6, 7, 8, 234–38, 298
concentration, 251, 271, 282
confidence, 5, 7, 8, 9, 71, 97, 100, 137, 237, 256, 298
consistency, 48, 49, 173, 190, 201, 250, 254, 256
core muscles, 249, 261–62, 273
Couples, Fred, 79
Crenshaw, Ben, 86, 108
cross lateral oblique crunch, 275–76
crunches, 249, 250, 273, 275–76
cues, visual, 92, 133–34, 158, 159, 185
curl, biceps, 269–71

Daly, John, 18, 75, 137
Daniel, Beth, 77, 87
David Leadbetter Academy, 61
Davies, Laura, 75, 137, 171, 183, 285
deltoid, 264–67
Diaz, Laura, 133, 249, 294
DiMarco, Chris, 77
disputes, resolving, 243–44
distance(s)
  control, 3, 52, 54, 97–98, 138, 197–98, 201, 233, 260
  evaluating, 230–32
divot
  playing from, 215–16
  tool, 295
double bogeys, 64, 136, 137, 156, 219, 239, 242
  see also bogeys
downhill lies, 211–12
downswing, 182–84
  biceps in, 269
  with irons, 201
  lats for, 259
  lunges for, 254
  obliques in, 275
  outer thigh lifts for, 257

squats for, 256
toe raises for, 258–59
draw, the, 207
drill(s), 31, 56, 58–65
  balance, 124–25
  ball position, 127
  break reading, 97
  follow-through, 91–92
  with gadgets, 50
  half-swing, 62, 63
  of iron shots, 201, 203
  one-foot, 52–54
  speed, 95–96
  swing, 88–89, 167, 191–95
  up-and-down, 64
drivers, 126, 127, 197–98, 203, 223
Duval, David
  crunches by, 250
  driving distance of, 75, 223
  grip of, 108, 109
  as solo player, 234
  swing of, 188–89, 190

eagle, 239, 242
Elkington, Steve, 56
Els, Ernie, 193, 250
Estes, Bob, 106, 110
etiquette, golf, 284–93
expectations, managing, 30–31
extensions, overhead, 268, 269

fairway woods. *See* woods, fairway
feel learning, 21–23
  of follow-through, 91
  by moving out and off, 54, 55
  practice and, 66
  putting and, 75, 78, 80
54 vision, 235
Finchem, Tim, 59
flagstick, 289–90
flexibility, 75, 179, 180, 198, 249, 250, 276
follow-through, 90–92
  in bunker shot, 162
  in chip shot, 138
  cutting off, 201, 203

follow-through (*continued*)
  with fairway woods, 204
  in lob shot, 152
  muscles for, 252
  in pitch shot, 147
  in power fade, 206
  in swing, 145, 188, 197
fourball match, 240–41
"fried egg," 157
front shoulder raise, 264–65
Futures Tour, 6

game(s)
  imaginary, 64
  nine-hole, 98
  playing the, 222–33
  putting, 97–99
  short, 71
  for two or more players, 238–43
Garcia, Sergio, 171
glutes, 252, 253–54
Goetz-Ackerman, Vicki, 75–76, 249
Grand Slam, 24
Green, Hubert, 21, 22, 272
green, moving off the, 55
grip, 77–81, 100–113
  with ball above feet, 212
  for chip shot, 143
  with fairway woods, 204
  feel of, 53
  in full swing, 168, 169, 171, 173, 174, 180
  interlocking, 107–9, 110
  for lob shot, 151
  overlapping, 108–9, 110
  for pitch shot, 146
  practice, 299
  preformed, 59–60
  ten-finger, 106–7, 110
  for uphill lie, 210
Gulbis, Natalie, 294

hammer curls, 269–71
hamstrings, 252, 253–54, 277–78
handicaps, 244–45
hands, strengthening the, 111–12

Harmon, Butch, 1, 196
high ball; low ball, 237
hitting, order of, 286–88
Hjertstedt, Gabriel, 223
Hogan, Ben
  on downswing, 183
  focus of, 236
  grip of, 102, 103
  practice by, 48, 227–28
  on setup, 124
Hogan, Valerie, 236
hole
  looking at, 91
  moving out from, 54, 58, 98
  starting at, 52–54
Howell, Charles III, 36
Howell, Charlie, 36
Howell, Debbie, 36

impact, moment of, 164, 165
  with ball above feet, 213
  to and beyond, 185–88
  clubface square at, 167–68
  in downhill lies, 211, 212
  draw and, 207
  with fairway woods, 204
  in knockdown shot, 206
  L angle and, 177, 180
  muscles and, 252
  in power fade, 206
  sweet spot and, 166–67
  tension and, 169–70
  unwinding toward, 182–84
injury, 65–66
Inkster, Juli, 86
instructor, choosing, 24, 28–29, 58
irons, 200–203
  for approach shot, 224
  ball position and, 126
  beginner, 45
  distances and, 230, 231, 232–33
  for knockdown shot, 206
  for one-more-club game, 238
  pros' use of, 223
  for recovery shot, 219

for scramble, 241
  for uphill lies, 210
Irwin, Hale, 272

Johnson, Trish, 285
Jones, Bobby, 102, 139
Junior National Ski Team, U.S., 3

Kane, Lori, 48–49, 86, 133, 249,
  262
kickbacks, triceps, 267–69
Kim, Mi Hyun, 18
King, Betsy, 13
Kite, Tom, 109

La Lanne, Jack, 274
L angle
  in backswing, 180, 195
  in downswing, 184, 269
  hands in, 147, 177
  at impact, 177, 182, 183, 188
lateral shoulder lift, 264, 265–66
lats, 259–61
Lauer, Matt, 37
Leadbetter, David, 1, 174
Leonard, Justin, 86, 250
lessons, 30–31, 58, 68, 299
Lickliter, Frank, 102
Lidback, Jenny, 60
lies, odd, 208–21
line
  in bunker shot, 158, 159, 162
  finding the, 130–33
  of putt, 93–96
  swing path and, 169–70
  through, 291
  see also target line
Lopez, Nancy
  ball position of, 126
  crunches by, 273
  on downswing, 183
  family of, 35
  as feel player, 22, 183
  grip of, 107
  thigh strength of, 254
Love III, Davis, 85

lower ab raises, 273–74
LPGA
  alignment checking in, 132
  Baugh in, 36, 198
  core muscles and, 249, 262
  Diaz in, 133
  Goetz-Ackerman in, 76
  Hall of Fame, 22, 108
  iron clubs in, 201
  Japanese, 6
  Kim in, 18
  Lidback in, 60
  Lopez in, 22
  match play in, 240
  Preisinger in, 107
  Rankin in, 108
  Reid in, 218–19
  Sorenstam in, 124, 235
  tees in, 98
Lumpkin, Jay, 8
lunges, 254–55

Masters Tournament, 196
McGann, Michelle, 183, 189
Mickelson, Phil, 52, 108
Mid-Amateur, 240
Miller, Alice, 13
Miller, Johnny, 36, 156
Modified Stableford, 242–43

NCAA, 76
Nelson, Byron, 217
Nelson, Larry, 272
net, hitting balls into, 194–95
net, indoor, 61
Nicklaus, Jack
  alignment and, 130, 133
  Beman and, 155
  on downswing, 183
  fitness and, 250, 254
  grip of, 103, 108
  on setup, 124
  on *Shell's Wonderful World of Golf*,
    290
  stroke of, 87
Norman, Greg, 133, 183, 250

O'Connor, Christie, Jr., 80
Oldfield, Ed, 4–5, 7, 14, 115

Pak, Se Ri
  ball position of, 126
  fitness program of, 249
  grip of, 109
  mistakes managed by, 48–49
  setup of, 116–17
  Sorenstam and, 235
  stroke of, 87
  as visual learner, 18
  waggle of, 171
Palmer, Arnold, 155, 191, 193, 290
"paralysis by analysis," 116
Penick, Harvey, 74, 75, 108, 109,
    174
Pepper, Dottie, 64, 87, 190
PGA Tour
  Beman on, 155
  Elkington on, 56
  Finchem on, 59
  fitness training on, 249–50
  Green on, 21
  home club of, 1–2, 223
  Lickliter on, 102
  match play on, 240
  Reid and, 223
  Sutton on, 109
  Woods on, 196
pin, attending the, 289–90
pivot, 178–82
plateauing, 297–98
Players Championship, 109
Players West Tour, 6
pledge, Cindy's front-nine, 299
points-system competition, 242–43
posture, 81–83
  Love III on, 85
  mirror and, 60
  for odd lies, 214
  pitch shot, 148
  setup, 115, 116–20, 122, 135, 141
  strengthening muscles for, 252, 262
practice, 48–71
  alignment, 132, 135

of bunker shot, 162
confidence from, 9
continued, 297
daily, 299
expectations and, 31
of flop shot, 155, 156
between lessons, 58
of pitch shot, 147
pitfalls, 65–68
before playing, 5
putting, 76–77, 97–99
scoring, 136–37, 162
of setup, 124–25
of shots, 138, 143
steady, incremental, 66, 68
of swing, 191–95
tips, 69–71
Preisinger, Carol, 107
President's Cup, 240
Price, Nick, 166
progress, evaluating, 71
push-ups, modified, 264
putter(s), putts, putting, 45,
    74–99
  flagstick and, 289–90
  follow-through on, 90–92
  glove-free, 80
  by Goetz-Ackerman, 75–76
  grip for, 77–81
  improving, 299
  indoor, 59
  long, 58, 95–96
  purchase of, 43–44
  reading, 93–96
  short, 96, 97–98
  slumps, 85
  watching your step while, 291
  see also putts, short
putts, short
  chip and, 138, 142, 143
  conceding, 239
  for distance control, 52, 53
  follow-through on, 90, 91
  grip for, 78
  lessons in, 58
  pitch and, 147

practice of, 71
for rhythm and timing, 54
up-and-down drill for, 64

quadriceps, 254–55, 278

Rankin, Judy, 34, 35, 108, 183
Rankin, Tuey, 35
Rawls, Betsy, 90
ready, being, 286–88
rear deltoid lift, 264, 266–67
reverse dips, 261–62
reverse rows, 259, 260, 261
rhythm
of follow-through, 91
movement and, 171
of pitch shot, 147
of putt, 75
of swing, 54, 59, 67, 119, 171, 173,
189, 190, 282
tension and, 171
of tour pros, 293
Robbins, Kelly, 79
Royal and Ancient Golf Club of
St. Andrews, 243–44
rubber bands, pulling, 112
Rules of Golf, The (USGA), 243
Ryder Cup, 240

scramble, 237, 241
scratch, 244
Seay, Ed, 290
Senior PGA Tour, 272
Senior U.S. Amateur, 240
setup, 114–35, 141–42
with ball below feet, 214
for divot, 215
with fairway woods, 203
for lob shot, 151, 152
mirror and, 60
muscles for, 252
for sand play, 157
stretching and, 276
for uphill lies, 209
Shell's Wonderful World of Golf
(TV program), 290

shots
alternate, 242
with ball above feet, 213
bump, 140
bunker, 136, 157–62
consistent, 250
diary of, 231, 232
difficult, 204, 206–7
draw, 207
explosion, 157–62
flop, 155–56
high-risk, 226–30
iron, 200 203
knockdown, 206
lob, 136, 151–54, 157
pitch, 58, 71, 136, 145–50, 151, 152,
159
power fade, 206–7
recovery, 136, 218–20
sand, 136, 157–62
scoring, 136–62
shank, 211, 291
short bump-and-run, 58
tee, 223, 224, 226, 241
thin, 186
shoulders
in backswing, 180, 252
strength training for, 253, 261,
264–67, 272, 275
stretch for, 280–81
Singh, Vijay
on backswing, 175
driving distance of, 223, 224
as friend, 37
grip of, 79
practice by, 49, 64, 71
putting length of, 75
swing of, 87, 189
"slot, the," 184
Solheim Cup, 240
Sorenstam, Annika, 50, 236
ball position of, 126
fitness program of, 249, 273
grip of, 79
setup of, 116, 124
swing of, 87, 188

Sorenstam, Annika *(continued)*
  on "54 vision," 235
  waggle of, 171
squats, 253–54, 256–57
stamina, 250, 251
Stephenson, Jan, 13, 79
strategy
  clothing investment, 45
  equipment investment, 45
  play, 31, 222–26, 239
  practice, 31, 68
strength, strength training, 75, 179,
    183, 198, 249, 250, 251–72
stretching, 249, 250, 276–81
stymies, 217
Sutton, Hall, 108, 109
sweet spot, 166–67
swing, 164–207
  alignment in, 130, 173
  balance and, 122
  with ball above feet, 212–13
  with ball below feet, 214–15
  ball position and, 127, 129
  in bunker shot, 159–62
  in chip shot, 156
  for divot, 215–16
  in downhill lies, 211, 212
  in draw, 207
  with fairway woods, 204
  freedom to, 119–20
  grip for, 100, 101, 103, 106–9, 111,
    113
  indoor, 60–61
  lessons before, 58
  in lob shot, 151
  more speed in, 250
  in one-more-club game, 237–38
  in pitch shot, 147, 156
  practice, 299
  preparation for, 55, 56
  quadriceps and, 254
  rhythm of, 119
  setup and, 114, 124
  sloppy, 65
  strength training for, 252, 256, 258,
    259–60, 265, 267–69

  in uphill lie, 210
  see also stroke
swing path, 169–70

takeaway, "one piece," 20–21, 174, 175,
    197
target line
  fairway woods and, 204
  in power fade, 206
  in swing, 165, 172, 173, 174, 175, 180,
    181, 185, 198
  from trouble spots, 221
technical learning, 23–24
tee(s)
  hitting, 193–94
  marking stroke with, 92
  in pockets, 295
  putting to, 98
  in reverse ladder, 97–98
  shots, 223, 224, 226, 241
tension, 169, 170–71, 174, 204
timing
  drill for, 197
  of pitch shot, 148
  posture and, 81
  of swing, 171, 173, 191, 195,
    282
Toski, Bob, 22
TPC Golf Schools, 8
  at Sawgrass, 1, 27, 33, 102
  at Scottsdale, 5
Trevino, Lee, 96
triceps, 253, 261, 267–69, 272,
    281
two-ball match, 236–37

uphill lies, 209–10
U.S. Amateur, 240
U.S. Open, 175
U.S. Women's Amateur, 75, 76
U.S. Women's Open, 76, 108
USGA (United States Golf
    Association), 34, 243, 244

Vardon, Harry, 102, 108
visual learning, 17–21

waggle(s), 171–73, 287
Walker Cup, 240
Walt Disney World Classic, 109
Watson, Tom, 90
Webb, Karrie
  ball position of, 126
  family of, 36
  grip of, 108
  practice by, 56–57, 58, 228
  Sorenstam and, 235
  swing of, 86, 190
  as technical learner, 24
  waggle of, 171
wedge(s)
  ball position and, 126, 127
  chipping with, 139
  for chip shot, 214, 217
  for flop shot, 155
  for fringe balls, 141
  lob, 145, 147
  for pitch shot, 45, 145, 147
  purchase of, 44
  for recovery shot, 220
  Reid's confiscation of, 140
  sand, 45, 145, 147, 155, 217
  in scramble, 241
weight training, 249, 250, 251–72
Women's World Long Drive, 56
Wonglukiet, Aree, 61

Wonglukiet, Naree, 61
woods, fairway, 203–4
  beginner, 45
  distances and, 230
  for fringe ball, 216
  for impossible shots, 226
  for knockdown shot, 206
  for recovery shot, 218, 219
Woods, Kultida, 36
Woods, Tiger, 50, 68
  on backswing, 175
  ball position of, 126
  on balls at fringe, 216
  grip of, 108, 110
  parents of, 36
  practice by, 228
  putting distance of, 75
  on setup, 124
  shots and, 137
  swing of, 86, 190, 196
  on television, 226
  as visual learner, 18
  waggle of, 171
  weights used by, 272
World Golf Village, 290

Zaharias, Babe, 102
Zubak, Jason, 125

Cindy Reid Golf™

Cindy Reid, Director of Instruction at the TPC at Sawgrass, home of the infamous 17th island green, offers a wide variety of golf instruction, including individual instruction, corporate outings, women's programs, junior programs, golf schools, short-game schools, Pro-for-the Day outings, motivational seminars, etiquette, rules, and course management training. For more information on these and other offerings please log on to CindyReidGolf.com or E-mail Cindy at creid4321@aol.com or call 1-800-556-5400 x3334.